Lincoln Christian College
A. C. Abrams
8031 Madison
St. Louis 14, Mo.

P9-DEF-213

The Orbits of Life

by

Jack Finegan

The Bethany Press

Saint Louis

COPYRIGHT, 1954

BY

THE BETHANY PRESS

Unless otherwise noted, Scripture quotations are from the Revised
Standard Version of the Bible, copyrighted 1946 and 1952 by the
Division of Christian Education, National Council of Churches, and
used by permission.

Printed in the United States of America

DCHS

To Dick on graduation from High School

Gates

5 March '87

74729

Preface

The chapters of this book are intended as essays for young people and others in present-day Christian thinking and Christian living. They endeavor to face squarely the problems of life in our time and place in world history, and they turn confidently to our Christian heritage, particularly as preserved in the Bible, for guidance. I hope they may convey something of the sense I have had in preparing them, of the discovery in Biblical records of long ago of truths which are amazingly fresh, relevant, and contemporary. Beginning with how individual life is perturbed and shadowed by apprehension in our time, I endeavor to lead the reader to a Biblical vantage point from which to look at the uncertainties of the years ahead and the confusions in our thought even now. Then I go on to the work to which Christians are called in our time, and to ways in which one finds strength and guidance for the doing of it. Since the book falls in the same series as my earlier *A Highway Shall Be There,* and *Like the Great Mountains,* I am glad that it also can be issued by The Bethany Press, and I express my appreciation to the Press for their interest and help in the publication.

JACK FINEGAN

Pacific School of Religion
Berkeley, California

Contents

The Orbits of Life

1. The Orbits of Life

In the thirteenth verse of the New Testament Book of Jude, certain persons of that time are spoken of as "wandering stars, to whom is reserved the blackness of darkness for ever."[1] This suggests that, like the heavenly bodies, lives have their orbits.

Wandering Comets

There is the orbit of life which is like that of the wandering comet. When Jude speaks about wandering stars he must be referring to what we know as comets, the strange visitors that appear in the sky from time to time. The ancient world was already considerably advanced in astronomical knowledge and was familiar with the existence of such bodies. One famous comet, for example, was that which appeared at the time when Julius Caesar died. As a matter of fact, our own word *comet* is derived directly from the Greek language in which these objects were referred to by the adjective *kometes* meaning "long-haired." A comet is a bright nucleus surrounded by a luminous fog technically designated as the coma, which blows out behind in a long streamer. The Greek designation for it was appropriate.

Several things may be said about the orbit of a wandering comet. For one, it is devoid of any central loyalty. The comet flashes in and curves around the sun, then rushes out and away into what Jude calls the "blackness of darkness for ever." It is influenced by the sun as it sweeps past, but it is not captured by it. Technically, the orbit may be a parabola or, more probably, a hyperbola. The parabola and hyperbola are conic sections which, respectively, equal or exceed unity. They are elongated orbits, on which the comet moves ever farther away. As it came near the sun there was a chance that it might have been captured—but it was not, and so it rushes on its way, unclaimed. It is life of that sort to which Jude refers.

Josiah Royce, the great philosopher, once said: "Unless you can find some sort of loyalty, you cannot find unity and peace in your active living." Some years ago in Florida a man attempted to assassinate President Roosevelt. When he was apprehended and interrogated, one question put to him was whether he belonged to a church. In reply to this he cried out, "No, no, I belong to nothing. I belong only to myself, and I suffer." This is the experience of a man unclaimed by any controlling loyalty.

This sort of an orbit of life is also disruptive in its influence upon others. Men have always tended to be afraid of comets, perhaps with reason. H. G. Wells once wrote a story entitled *The Star*, in which he pictured a tremendous heavenly body rushing directly toward the earth. Fear spread everywhere as it looked more and more certain that there would be complete catastrophe. Even though at last the star was deflected and utter annihilation did not result, there was still widespread devastation. A more recent book, *Worlds in Collision* by Immanuel Velikovsky, was based on the theory that in the second millennium B.C. a great comet came within our solar system and close to the earth, causing plagues in Egypt, parting of the Red Sea, floods in China, and a multitude of other things which I suspect did not all happen at the same time, but were fitted together to make this hypothesis impressive. At all events, a comet can be a disruptive influence, and that is what Jude says is the case with the lives of people who are like wandering stars.

In that day some of these people seem to have been right within the circles of the church, for he speaks of them as "spots in your feasts of charity."[2] Evidently they did not hesitate to disrupt even the most sacred fellowship by their wild wanderings. Of all places upon earth it is in a church that there should be a demonstration of the charity which is taught by Jesus Christ, and if instead there is whispering behind people's backs, fomenting of trouble, and lack of cooperation, it is most regrettable. Out in the world also there are unscrupulous persons, drug peddlers and others, who do not hesitate to lead astray with themselves as many others as they can. Such is the disruptive influence of this kind of life.

Furthermore, when life moves in such an orbit, it is destined for darkness. It is thus with wandering comets. The great comet of 1882 disappeared in the direction of the star Sirius. Although Sirius is one of the nearer stars it is still very distant. It was calculated that it would take the comet 140 million years to travel from our sun to Sirius. It would then flash by and go on out into further emptiness and darkness. F. R. Moulton says in his *Introduction to Astronomy* that if the comets do wander from star to star, they spend most of their time in traveling and little in visiting. Of the kind of life which Jude describes, which is never claimed by anything and which does not hesitate to leave a wake of destruction behind it, it may be said that if it keeps on going on such a course it is destined for the blackness of darkness forever.

Periodic Comets

There are also periodic comets. These likewise go rushing out into space, but never quite escape the pull of the sun, and at last come back again. These comets travel not in a hyperbola or a parabola but in an ellipse. This means that they will not ever escape the gravitational field of the sun but, at a remote distance, will still be held by it and pulled back again. A partial table lists more than thirty periodic comets, the orbits of which have been charted. Of these the best known is Halley's Comet. This body derived its name from Halley, a friend of Newton, who calculated its orbit from observations made in 1682. He found the orbit to be almost identical with orbits of comets that had come in 1607 and 1531. Since there was a period of approximately seventy-five years intervening each time, he concluded that this must be the same comet returning at such intervals, and he predicted that it would come back again in 1759. In that year, within a month of the time he predicted, the comet was again in the sky. The last time it visited us was in 1910 when it was at perihelion (nearest the sun) on April 20. Then it started rushing out, away and away, and in the astronomy books you can see charts showing its tremendous elliptical course. Going out past the orbits of Mars, Jupiter, Saturn, and Uranus, it crossed the orbit of Neptune on January 1, 1930. On January 1, 1950, this comet was farthest out and apparently still rushing on into the emptiness of darkness forever. But not so. Far, immensely far out there, the pull of the sun was still holding it and slowing its outward rushing and bending and curving it around, and now it is commencing to come back—it is rushing back—and on April 29, 1986, it will again be in perihelion, nearest to the sun.

This also is an orbit of life. While the illustration will hardly fit at all points, it is a fact that a person may be able to tear himself away from God and thrust himself far, far out into regions of darkness, and yet, even there, not be able to get away from where God still exerts an attracting force upon him. From far out there he may still be able to turn and get back to God before it is too late. There are people like this. Zacchaeus was one in the New Testament. How far he had gone! But Jesus came to him and brought him back again. The dying thief on the cross beside Christ was one of these—almost on the edge of darkness; but still the kind of love that was God's love, that was in Jesus Christ, exerted its force upon him and in the last moments brought him back.

Some astronomers think that all comets will at last return. This would mean that all of them travel in ellipses rather than parabolas or hyperbolas. Since from the earth we are able to observe only a very small segment of their total orbit, it is possible that our observations are not accurate enough to be able to know. It may be that all of them will at last come back. Certainly our observations of human life are not accurate enough to justify us in saying about any person that he is so far on his way out from God that he will never get back again. We do not comprehend all the infinite goodness and power of God, and we do not know if one who now seems to be going utterly away from him will at long last feel the pull and recognize the power of God's love and come back once again.

Circling Planets

There is yet a third kind of orbit of life, and that is suggested by the orbit of the circling planets. To be sure, the planets themselves are not traveling in perfect circles, and perhaps no human being will ever trace out an orbit of life which is perfectly regular and without deviation. Although the planets travel in ellipses, these are much more nearly perfect circles, and whereas the comets are bizarre and unstable, the planets are relatively stable and simple in motion. On these planets, at least on our earth, life is possible.

The planets circling around the sun are controlled by a central power and radiant with the reflection of a central glory. How splendid is life when it is like this. It is a great thing when a person is captured by an idea. Felix Adler says, "I am grateful for the Idea that has used me." It is a great thing when a person is captured by the work that he is destined to do. John Masefield became the poet laureate of England, but at one time he was a very ordinary youth working in a factory. Tending a machine all day long, with contradictory impulses within himself, no inspiration was apparent, no far horizon beckoned. Then as he read books, he began to fall under their spell. Finally he discovered Keats, and he says that then for the first time he knew that his own life belonged to poetry. It is a great thing when something captures us and holds us, and in our work and lives we come to reflect its splendor and radiance.

It is a great thing when the power of God and power of Christ capture and hold us. In one of the Psalms it is said, "The Lord God is a sun."[3] His power, accepted as the center of life, can hold us steady. Of Jesus Christ we sing, "Sun of my soul, thou Saviour dear, it is not night if thou be near." It is light indeed when our lives are in an orbit controlled by him and illuminated by his glory. He has died for us, and there is power in that fact to pull us and to hold us. Russell Conwell, once an army captain and later the

famous Philadelphia preacher and author of the widely
heard lecture, "Acres of Diamonds," was converted
when he found that his orderly, John Ring, had laid
down his life for him. He said, "When I stood beside
the body of John Ring and realized that he had died
for the love of me, I made a vow that has formed my
life. I vowed that from that moment I would live not
only my own life, but I would also live the life of John
Ring. And from that moment I have worked sixteen
hours a day, eight hours for John Ring's work and
eight hours for my own."

Christ has died for all of us. It is a great thing to
be captured by him and then to become an influence on
his behalf upon others. The remark of a Boston newspaper about Phillips Brooks has never been forgotten:
"It was a dull rainy day when things looked dark and
lowering, but Phillips Brooks came down through
Newspaper Row and all was bright." Hillis wrote:
"We watch with wonder the apparent flight of the sun
through space, glowing upon dead planets, shortening
winter and bringing summer, with birds, leaves and
fruits. But that is not half so wonderful as the passage
of a human heart, glowing and sparkling with ten
thousand effects, as it moves through life. The soul,
like the sun, has its atmosphere and is over against its
fellows, for light, warmth, and transformation." That
is the mission of a Christian as he moves in a life orbit
controlled by Christ.

2. It May Not Be as Late as You Think

In Mark 13:7 a word of Jesus is recorded which brings appropriate encouragement to our own apprehensive time: "And when you hear of wars and rumors of wars, do not be alarmed; this must take place, but the end is not yet."

Expecting the End

Some of us go through life constantly thinking that the end is at hand. Men have often been apprehensive of the end of the world. As the early followers of Jesus witnessed social convulsions in their time, many of them felt the absolute end was signaled. This word told them that those things had to take place and that it was not necessarily the end. The Thessalonian Christians were worried about the same thing. In A.D. 50 they thought the end was at hand. The letters which Paul wrote to them were occasioned by and occupied with this problem. Some of the Thessalonians stopped working, and Paul said to them that if anyone would not work, he should not eat. Others were anxious about their loved ones who had already died: they had the terrible feeling that these had died just too soon, and were going to miss out on the wonderful second coming of Christ, which would happen at any moment.   So Paul tried to comfort them and reassure them on that score.   Others, strangely enough, believed that the end had already taken place, and because of that they felt free to do anything they wanted. Paul had to straighten them out on that, too.

We also have often had the apprehension that the decline of civilization is upon us.   This feeling has been particularly prevalent since Oswald Spengler wrote his famous work on the *Decline of the West*.   Since that time we have watched nervously and anxiously for the signs of the fulfillment of this predicted downfall.   A more recent book was entitled *Five Minutes to Twelve*. We wonder if we are actually that near to midnight.

Again and again there has been anxious apprehension in relation to war, and this is small enough wonder, for most of us can hardly remember when there was not the threat of war or actual war.   In the presence of this anxiety some of us have been tempted to do the same thing that the Thessalonian Christians did—drop everything.   What is the use of anything?   The end is almost here.   Why stay in school?   Why make plans?   Why go ahead with work?   It is very late.

Also, we often experience apprehension in relation to the loss of health.   Almost all of us occasionally manifest symptoms of disease, or acquire actual diseases.   Many of us are thereupon inclined to feel that the end is near. Such anxiety about the loss of health has darkened many days.

We have been fearful, moreover, about the coming of old age. A freshman in college, having graduated from high school, lamented his lost youth. A person in the twenties searched for signs of his senility and advertised his antiquity. All of us, with each further decade, may be assailed by the feeling that we are just on the edge of being old and that it is about all over for us.

What Actually Happens

What actually happens is often better than what is anticipated in advance. The end does not come on the schedule we have assumed it will follow. Of course it is not to be denied that the end will ultimately take place. The end of the world will come someday; before that our civilization may decline. The ruin of war is devastating a part of the earth even now. The physical mechanism of human life will wear out. Age, as measured by the calendar, comes inexorably. None of this is denied. But it is observed here that, again and again, when men make schedules in the attitude of apprehension and anticipate that complete darkness is at hand, it does not happen that way.

The end of the world has not yet taken place. In 1843, William Miller, a very earnest and devoted student of the Scriptures, pondered the meaning of Daniel 8:14, in which Daniel mentions 2,300 days. As he thought about it, it seemed clear to Miller that that really meant 2,300 years. It also occurred to him that the point from which to begin counting was the return of Ezra to Jerusalem in 457 B.C. So he counted 2,300 years from 457 B.C. and arrived at the date of A.D. 1843. The people to whom he announced the result were naturally electrified. A great many of them did the same thing that the Thessalonian Christians did: they dropped everything and waited for the end. But it did not take place. Then, upon further study, Miller decided that he had been in error because he had calculated by the Hebrew method of chronology rather than by the Roman. Upon revising his figures accordingly, he secured the date of 1844. So again men waited through the year, and again the end did not take place. Of course the end of the world will transpire sometime, but probably not when we calculate that it will. Jesus said that it will come like a thief in the night. Thieves have an unhappy facility in coming when you do not expect them. Thus it will be with the end.

Civilization's day of apparent doom has sometimes been in reality civilization's new day. The most lugubrious statements have been made by eminent authorities and completely contradicted by the actual course of events. In 1839 a Congressman from Mississippi said: "Our system is finished; opportunity has already disappeared from among us." In 1844 a commissioner of patents declared: "We see the arrival of that period when human improvement is at an end." In 1875 a commissioner of the interior announced: "Scientific invention can take us only a little way further." Imagine

throwing up your hands and resigning yourself to discouragement in 1875 because science had reached its
frontier and there was not anything more to be accom-
plished! Again and again the greatest progress has
taken place at the very time when men have decided
that there would be no more progress.

What shall I say about war? I have often enough
told how terrible it is, called it the greatest evil of our
civilization, and viewed it with apprehension and alarm.
War is a terrible thing. Yet even here it is true there
can be exaggeration. Fewer people perished on earth
in all the hostilities of the first and second world wars
than lost their lives in the influenza epidemic of 1918.
Fewer Americans were killed and wounded on the
battlefield in the second world war than on the high-
ways of the United States. Of all those who were in-
jured in the war, 97 per cent recovered their health.
Therefore if there is any young man or young woman
tempted because of apprehension of war to throw
everything overboard, it is unwise. One may bring
irrevocable ruin upon oneself by such action, when the
ruin that one fears might not be so all-encompassing
as in anxious apprehension one anticipates ahead of
time.

As for the loss of health, health is not only lost, it is
also gained and regained. William O. Douglas has
written *Of Men and Mountains*. Reading this book,
we walk beneath the snow-clad peaks of the Northwest
—Rainier and Adams and the others—and in the
pleasant valleys amidst these mountains—Klickitat

Meadows, North Minam Meadows and the rest—and meet some of the friends of the author. North Minam Meadows are described as a place of ice-cold springs, and groves of trees suitable for camping. There from May until August most of the wild flowers of the Wallowas flourish, and in late June the snowbush fills the valley with its fragrance. The friend whose life-story was closely wrapped up with this meadow was Joseph C. Culbertson. It was there that he came to die. He acquired a lung infection from research in chemistry, and the doctors gave him six months to live. As he lay in his bed trying to think where he wanted to spend those last few months, he remembered North Minam Meadows. He managed to get there. For a long time he lay in a screened-in tent. But then he began to go fishing. He went back for four successive seasons. It was there that Douglas met him in health, six years after he had gone there to die.

A newspaper columnist told about Gerald Kersh, the British novelist. He was operated on at the University of Pennsylvania Hospital for a disease so serious that a portion of the removed liver was put on display in the museum of pathology. The doctors expressed little hope for his recovery. When his secretary came in, she was much affected to see him so sick. He said that they would have to do something about getting funeral expenses ready and, as much to calm her as anything else, dictated a 17,500-word novel. He sold this to *The Saturday Evening Post*, recovered, and sailed for home!

What about getting old?   By the calendar that assuredly takes place, and yet even here it is possible that "the best is yet to be."   This phrase is from a poem by Browning, and has recently been used as the title of a book.   One story in the book is of an eighty-seven-year-old woman who made an appointment with a social worker to discuss requirements for admission to a home for the aged.   She arrived on time for the appointment, but had thought she might be late because her plane had encountered rough weather on the way from Florida.   The social worker said that it would not have mattered because another hour could have been arranged.   The eighty-seven-year-old woman explained, however, that she had to catch another plane at four o'clock that same day to Boston.   By now the social worker was wondering whether a person as active and vigorous as this would be content to stay in a home for the aged.   She informed him, however, that it was not for herself at all.   She would not consider it.   It was for her niece, she said, who was getting old and concerning whom she was quite anxious.   The social worker asked the niece's age, and was told that she would be sixty-six on her next birthday!

An unknown author has written:

> Youth is not a time of life;
> It is a state of mind.
>> It's not a matter of ripe lips and supple knee,
>> A temper of the will,
>> A quality of the imagination,
>> A vigor of the emotions.
> It's the freshness of the deep spring of life.

Nobody grows old by simply living a number of years.
People grow old by losing their ideals.
  Years wrinkle the skin;
  But to give up enthusiasms wrinkles the soul.
  Worry, doubt, self-distrust, fear, despair,
  These are the long, long years that bow the heart
And turn the greening spirit back to dust.

Whether sixty or sixteen,
There should be in every human being's heart
  The lure of wonder,
  The sweet amazement of the stars,
  The starlike things and thoughts,
  The undaunted challenge of events,
  The unfailing appetite for what's next,
And the joy in the game of living.

You are as young as your hope,
And as old as your doubt;
  As young as your self-confidence,
  As old as your fear.
  In the central place of your heart is a wireless station.
  So long as it receives messages of hope, beauty, love,
    courage, cheer
And the love of God and your fellow-men, you are
    young.

In the central place of your heart
  Is an evergreen tree;
  So long as it flourishes,
  You are young.
  When it dies,
You are old.

Jesus' Way Is the Way

So it is that we come to the inescapable conclusion that the statement of Jesus is absolutely true and tells us the way to live: "And when you hear of wars and rumors of wars, do not be alarmed . . . the end is not yet." The wisdom of God is beyond our finding out. The universe of God is inexhaustible. The surprises of God are wonderful. History is habitually unpredictable. So long as there is life, there is hope. Do not quit too soon. Do not get tired too soon. Do not lose interest too soon. Fear brings the end, but faith opens new beginnings. Live by faith and hope and love. This is the only way of life in God's ever surprising world. When you hear of things that tend to strike fear to the heart, endeavor not to be unduly troubled. Such things must be, but it may be that the end is not yet.

3. The Realism of the Bible

The word *realism* means telling about things as they actually are. It is commonly opposed to the term *idealism*. In the philosophy of Plato, for example, idealism is the doctrine that ideas are the most real thing, and that what we have here on earth is just a shadow of that. Realism is also opposed to romanticism, which means dealing with things in such an exaggerated and sentimental way that you do not actually see them as they are. Realism is seeing things as they actually are, seeing things as if a clear light fell upon them. In Psalm 119:105 it is declared: "Thy word is a lamp to my feet and a light to my path." I am sure that the Bible is idealistic in the sense that it points us to what is above and beyond; and it is even romantic, if you please, in the deathless devotions with which it deals. But most of all we may affirm that it is realistic, in that it casts a clear light upon things as they actually are.

What Actually Happened

The Bible tells us how things have actually happened in history. It is a verifiable record of actual events. It fits into the background of its world. It checks with what we find when we go into the world out of which it came. If we are told that the Bible contains myth and legend and history, that is not surprising for in the ancient world all three of these were ways of conveying truths. But the part that is historical is a very large part of the Bible. It certainly tells a great many things which actually happened in history. The more we learn about the history of the ancient Near East in general, the more we realize that the Bible fits into it. The more we proceed with archeological work in particular, the more we find detailed points of correlation. Several examples of these may now be given. It may be that no single one of them will seem of major importance, yet all put together, they are of the sort which combine to give a new impression of the historical value of the Bible. If any of us have been inclined to read the Bible as a book about which there is an air of unreality and which deals with a never-never land of make-believe, we should deal with such facts as these. For the Bible has to do with real places and events.

As one peruses the story of Abraham in the Old Testament, one comes upon mention of the children of Heth. Only a few years ago nobody had any idea who the children of Heth were; they could have been a purely imaginary people. Now we recognize that the children of Heth of the Old Testament are none other than the Hittites, some of whose cities have been excavated, some of whose literature has been recovered, who had a great empire and were an important people.

In the Old Testament one also comes upon the Horites. These too were an otherwise unknown people only a few years ago. Now we realize that the Horites are none other than the Hurrians, a people concerning whom much has been learned in recent years, and of whose laws and customs much is now known. Interestingly enough, these Hurrian laws and customs appear to be the very same kind as are reflected in some of the narratives about the patriarchs of the Old Testament.

Then consider the matter of the coming of the children of Israel into Palestine, their Promised Land. One might imagine that these stories were invented in order to justify some ancient claim to the country. But actually there are many correlations between what the Bible tells and what has been found in the city mounds of Palestine. For example, the Bible tells about the taking of the city of Jericho by the Israelites. When Jericho was excavated, it was found that the ancient city walls had actually fallen out and down the mound. In the Bible is a record of the taking of the city of Lachish by the Israelites. When this city mound was dug down through to just about the depth that would correspond to a period that far back in history, there was a layer of ashes remaining from the conflagration in which the city was destroyed. When Debir was excavated, there was evidence of the destruction of that city at about the same time. At present it looks as if Jericho fell somewhat earlier than Lachish and Debir, so the taking of Palestine may have been a more complicated and more drawn-out undertaking than might be assumed from some of the condensed Biblical statements; nevertheless the general impression is unmistakable: the Bible is dealing with real events.

The Bible also presents vivid pictures of real people. If at the outset, early mankind is personified in the figures of Adam, meaning man, and Eve, meaning life, or mother of the living, that is only what might be expected of a poetic author. Before long we come upon the personages of Abraham and his immediate descendants. Of them an eminent archeologist says: "The figures of Abraham, Isaac, Jacob, and Joseph appear before us as real personalities, each one of whom shows traits and qualities which suit his character but would not harmonize with the characters of the others."[1] When later we read of Saul in his melancholia, of David with his winsomeness and weakness, and of Solomon with his love of luxury and ostentation, we know that these are real people, vividly portrayed.

In the Bible there is also a vital account of the real life of the Founder of Christianity. The various books and letters of the New Testament were written in order to help people in practical problems, and in order to bring people to faith in the living Christ. But they did that by telling what had actually taken place in history. The spirit in which they were written is expressed in 2 Peter 1:16: "For we did not follow cunningly devised fables, when we made known unto you the power and coming of our Lord Jesus Christ, but we were eyewitnesses of his majesty."[2]

In his book on *The Man From Nazareth*, Harry Emerson Fosdick remarks that, broadly speaking, there are two kinds of religion in the world, one based upon historic founders, the other centered around mythological personalities. Religions with historic founders include Buddhism which originated with Gautama Buddha, Zoroastrianism which was founded by Zoroaster, Islam which came from the teachings of Muhammad, and Judaism which rests upon the law of Moses. Other religions grew up around such mythical figures as Jupiter, Juno, Isis, Osiris, Mithras, and Dionysus. To which type does Christianity belong? It is the kind of religion that started because there was a real person in history as its founder. Dr. Fosdick puts it thus: "Does mythology construct a god by picturing a man like this: a carpenter by trade, loving flowers and children, talking about garments that need patching and about poor folk buying two sparrows for a penny; telling stories in a style so characteristically his own that they cannot be reduplicated; being weary and hungry and angry and out of heart; called 'beside himself' by his family, a heretic by his church, a traitor by his government? This is not the way mythical gods are made."[3]

How Life Is

But the Bible is not only a lamp shedding its light back into history, it is also a light for the present. It shows how things are here and now. It tells us how things are as we go along through life. As a matter of fact, we often do not appreciate the Bible until we encounter for ourselves some of the experiences of which it speaks. Then, in the light of personal knowledge, we realize that the Bible had contained the truth about the matter all along. Until we have some trouble in life ourselves, how can we understand the Book of Job? Until we experience inner struggle, how can we understand Paul and his words about wanting to do good, but finding that he has done evil instead?

How relevant the Bible is to the various experiences of life appears in this list of suggested readings by Professor Harris Franklin Rall:

> When in sorrow, read John 14.
> When men fail you, read Psalm 27.
> When you have sinned, read Psalm 51.
> When you worry, read Matthew 6:19-34.
> Before church service, read Psalm 84.
> When you are in danger, read Psalm 91.
> When you have the blues, read Psalm 34.
> When God seems far away, read Psalm 139.
> When you are discouraged, read Isaiah 40.
> If you want to be fruitful, read John 15.
> When doubts come upon you, try John 7:17.
> When you are lonely or fearful, read Psalm 23.
> When you forget your blessings, read Psalm 103.
> For Jesus' idea of a Christian, read Matthew 5.
> For James's idea of religion, read James 1:19-27.
> When your faith needs stirring, read Hebrews 11.
> When you feel down and out, read Romans 8:31-39.
> When you want courage for your task, read Joshua 1.
> When the world seems bigger than God, read Psalm 90.
> When you want rest and peace, read Matthew 11:25-30.

When you want Christian assurance, Romans 8:1-30.
For Paul's secret of happiness, read Colossians 3:12-17.
When you leave home for labor or travel, Psalm 121.
When you grow bitter or critical, read 1 Corinthians 13.
When your prayers grow narrow or selfish, Psalm 67.
For Paul's idea of Christianity, read 2 Corinthians 5:15-19.
For Paul's rules on how to get along with men, Romans 12.
When you think of investments and returns, Mark 10:17-31.
For a great invitation and a great opportunity, Isaiah 55.
For Jesus' idea of prayer, Luke 11:1-13.
For the prophet's picture of worship that counts, Isaiah 58:1-12.
For the prophet's idea of religion, Micah 6:6-8.

After looking at such a list we can appreciate the wisdom of the further suggestion: "Why not follow Psalm 119:11 and hide some of these in your memory?"[4]

It is small wonder that Henry Hallam said: "I see that the Bible fits into every fold and crevice of the human heart. I am a man, and I believe that this is God's Book because it is man's book." And that Coleridge remarked: "I know the Bible is inspired because it finds me at a greater depth of my being than any other book."

What Will Be

The light of the Bible shines also into the future. Since it tells reliably what happened in the past, and since it shows dependably how life is in the present, we have good reason to believe that it is also realistic in what it tells about the future. Here are just three of its offers and promises: The first is salvation. The Bible teaches that if any man believes in Jesus Christ he shall be saved. The second promise is that the faithful Christian will be taken care of in trial and temptation. God is faithful, and will not allow us to be tempted above our ability to withstand, but with the temptation will provide also the way out. The third guarantee is that of everlasting life. To those who dedicate themselves to the doing of good with patience, and thereby seek after honor and glory and immortality, God will give eternal life. These are the promises, and they are as good as the great Book in which they are written and as the gracious God from whom they come.

4. The Second Half of the Century

The second half of the twentieth century is unfolding. When we endeavor to discern the shape of things to come in it, we are much like Moses standing on the mountain and gazing across into Palestine. According to the Book of Deuteronomy, Moses ascended Mount Pisgah, and from its summit viewed western Palestine. Then, in the light of what he envisioned as the alternatives before his people as they moved across into that land of promise, he uttered these words to them: "I have set before you life and death, blessing and curse; therefore choose life, that you and your descendants may live."[1] Again and again what is enacted in the Bible seems to come alive and be enacted anew in our time. What transpired in Bible times may have taken place on a small scale geographically and in the number of people involved, but now the same thing comes to pass again on a world scale and with all mankind involved. On the edge of the unknown land of the second half of our century, looking across into it, trying to recognize the alternatives which confront us, it almost seems as if the stern and stirring voice of Moses were speaking again. His words almost sound as if they were directed specifically to us.

Death and Curse

On the one hand, according to the statement of Moses, there is the prospect of death and curse. Is that true in the second half of this century? It is abundantly and terribly true, according to many of our most prominent prophets. One aspect of the death that may overtake us in the second half of the twentieth century is that there may be totalitarianism everywhere. A satirical description of such a probable state of affairs was written by George Orwell in a book entitled *Nineteen Eighty-Four*. Writing in 1949, he looked ahead thirty-five years to see the final consummation of the trend toward totalitarianism. The picture is not pleasant. In it the world is divided into three superstates: East Asia, Eurasia, and Oceania. Each one is a colossal totalitarian system that maintains its being by constant antagonism with another such system. The system maintains its force at home because it is founded upon hate against those without. The pathetic hero of the book, Winston Smith, is an average man, or perhaps something a bit better than that, since he is a member of the Party. He works in the Ministry of Truth. His business there is to keep going back into the newspapers and records of the past and changing them so they agree with what the Party says today. He lives in Victory Mansions. On the wall of his drab apartment is a telescreen. It both receives and transmits, so when he stands in front of it in the morning to perform his morning exercises, he sees his instructor and his instructor sees him. When he fails to touch his toes as vigorously as he ought, the instructor barks out his name and number and exhorts him to greater calisthenic zeal. Outside the window hovers the helicopter of the Police, snooping. The agents of the Thought Police are unrecognizable—they may be anywhere; your best friend may be one of them. Every day the radio broadcasts two minutes of Hate, the purpose of which is to maintain the frenzy of feeling against the enemy so that the regime may continue at home. Posters everywhere carry the picture of the leader of the Party and the slogan, "Big Brother Is Watching You." The mottos of the Party are ceaselessly reiterated: "Freedom Is Slavery"; "War Is Peace"; "Ignorance Is Strength." To have such a system as this prevailing everywhere on earth would indeed be death and a curse. Not a few refugees have risked their lives to leave Europe rather than to continue to live under such a system.

Self-destruction is another aspect of the death and curse which some envision as a distinct possibility, if not a major probability, in the second half of the century. Philip Wylie has written a story called *Blunder*. It takes place in the 1970's. At that time, according to the story, two scientists carry out certain calculations on the binding fractions of bismuth. In the calculations they make a mistake. Three other scientists perceive the error and realize that if the experiment the two have projected is carried out, it will result not in setting up a limited controlled reaction but rather in setting loose a global chain reaction. The three scientists are desperately trying to head off the performance of the experiment when the two others proceed to carry it out. As a result, an unlimited global chain reaction is set off, the earth splits like a melon, and is totally vaporized in one nineteenth of a second. If Moses spoke about death and curse, what he could foresee must have been on a very small scale as compared with what scientific judgment envisions as a distinct possibility within the second half of our century.

Diabolical religion is another aspect of the death and curse which some think probable before this century is over. Aldous Huxley has written an ugly book called *Ape and Essence,* in which he undertakes to picture what happens at the end of the century. A terrible war devastates most of the earth; then after the radioactivity dissipates sufficiently to make it possible, an expedition comes from New Zealand to rediscover America. It is in A.D. 2108 when the party arrives off the coast of California. New Zealand itself had not been destroyed, not for any humanitarian reason, but simply because of its remoteness. The scientists of that land had therefore been able to organize this New Zealand Rediscovery Expedition to America. On the coast of southern California they found the wretched and miserable survivors of the third World War, and their children, living among the ruins of what had been a great city. In all the revolting picture of their life, perhaps the most terrible part is the diabolical religion to which they have resorted. Time was when men saw so many good things in the world that they believed in a good God. These people had seen so many evil things happen that they were driven to believe in an evil Devil as the ruler of the universe, and they worshiped him in fear and loathing. It would indeed be death and curse, if religion, which should sustain us, were to become the source of our defeat. Totalitarianism, self-destruction, diabolical religion—what Moses could see by way of disaster and trouble for his people as he looked across into Palestine was certainly not more terrible than what some of our prophets picture as a distinct possibility in the second half of our century.

Life and Blessing

But Moses saw another alternative: he saw the possibility of life and of blessing. And so do we. What amazing possibilities of blessing and of life there are ahead, in the second half of our century—possibilities as immensely more wonderful as the terror is immensely more terrible. There is the possibility of a revitalized democracy. The very threat of totalitarianism in our day may drive us back again to the real foundations of democracy, and constrain us to build anew upon those foundations. What are the foundations? They certainly include faith in God, for the people who built our country, who crossed the ocean to come to it and crossed the deserts to come to the West, were people animated and inspired by faith in God and in his purpose. Foundational, too, was the belief that every person matters, the belief that every human individual possesses an inalienable dignity. We must go back again to such foundations and then build upon them such a life as will bring to all the people the reality of democracy. Mr. Herbert Hoover has remarked that at about the same time that Hegel, and a little later, Karl Marx, were setting forth their philosophy of agnosticism and their belief that the individual is just a slave and puppet of the state and that his rights are derived from the state, our ancestors were proclaiming that the Creator has endowed all mankind with free will and with rights of freedom as children of God. He declared that the despair of Europe today comes from the one philosophy, and the greatness of America from the other. So it is a distinct possibility that the very threat of totalitarianism will drive us, not to an ever increasing imitation of totalitarianism, but rather to an affirmation of what democracy is, and an extension of its true nature to all the people who want to have a share in it. This would mean life, this would mean blessing for many people.

What if the second half of our century holds also the blessings of a constructively employed science? Wonderful things have transpired in the past half century in this regard. In 1939 the *Wall Street Journal* looked back over the preceding ten years and drew up a list of some of the things that had not been known in 1929 but were familiar then. The list included: streamlined trains, television, transoceanic passenger air service, synthetic rubber, fluorescent lighting, colored home movies, plywood stronger than steel, half a dozen new plastics and resins, polarized glass, glass building blocks, fiber glass for insulation and textiles, synthetic hosiery, and synthetic vitamins. In 1949 the Institute of Life Insurance glanced back over the preceding decade and reported these advances on the front of health: in 1949 the death rate from communicable diseases of childhood was one-fourth that of ten years before; that for influenza and pneumonia was down 60 per cent; tuberculosis was down 45 per cent. What amazing and wonderful strides have been made within these two recent decades! Remember, also, that there is a tendency in scientific progress for acceleration, for a constant speeding up of the process as knowledge builds up. What life and blessing can come to multitudes of people within the second half of the century if science be used for constructive purposes!

What if, furthermore, instead of diabolical religion, we should have a united Christianity bringing to bear upon the life of the world the full power of the Christian gospel? There is a distinct possibility, perhaps now even a definite probability, that this will come to pass within the next half century. When the topic, "Should the Protestant churches unite now?" was debated on a recent national radio program, those who planned the program expected a routine response. They were surprised when they received the largest response from the listeners for any program for the entire year. Of all those who wrote in, 94.8 per cent said that they favored a united Protestant church now. President Henry Van Dusen of Union Theological Seminary has expressed this judgment: "I do not say that we shall soon have one big single Protestant Church. I do foresee, within this century, the merging of most of the largest of the present 250 separate Protestant communions into six to eight major church bodies, and these so linked together that they will be virtually unified in much of their Christian work and influence. That is the direction in which we are moving."[2]

See, then, how the alternatives line up over against each other: totalitarianism or a revitalized democracy; self-destruction by technology, or science at work in constructive ways for the welfare of mankind; a diabolical religion, or a unified Christianity with mighty power, bringing the gospel of salvation to the world. If Moses saw life and death, blessing and curse ahead, we do too. Indeed the life and death, the blessing and curse, seem to be on a larger scale than ever before, with more terrible possibilities on the one side than mankind ever had to confront previously, and with more dazzlingly wonderful possibilities on the other hand than mankind ever dared to envision before. The modern philosopher, Ralph Barton Perry, spoke truly when he said that we have to choose between a worse evil and a greater good than mankind has ever known before.

Therefore Choose

What did Moses say to do about it? He said, "Therefore choose life, that you and your descendants may live." The word *choose* provides the clue. There is a live option here. The outcome is yet to be decided, and we have the power of choice. God's providence is certainly at work, but in it he has allotted to man the ability to discern between alternatives and to act. The atoms cannot choose, the stars cannot, but man can. Whenever man chooses to take a single step in the direction of God's purpose, then God walks with him and smooths that way, bringing him on toward the blessing that is possible. Upon our choices, therefore, and upon the choices of other people just like ourselves, will hinge and hang the destiny of the second half of the century. A choice for God will bring life and blessing, for us and our world.

5. Religion: Confusionism

Dr. E. Stanley Jones tells of a Chinese student in the Straits Settlements, not yet too familiar with the English language, who filled out a church registration card and wrote in the blank which called for his religion the word Confusionism. If all of us were completely honest, probably some of the rest of us would state our faith in the same way: Religion, Confusionism.

Areas of Confusion

There is confusion today in the philosophy of religion. This is where we endeavor to think about our faith. As long as we accept it unquestioningly we avoid difficulty, but when we consider it critically we encounter perplexity.

> The centipede was happy quite, until the toad in fun
> Said, "Pray which leg comes after which when you
>   begin to run?"
> This wrought his mind to such a pitch
> He lay distracted in a ditch
> Uncertain how to run.

When we make inquiries about the philosophy of religion we find at least eight major points of view competing for our allegiance. These are the philosophies of Roman Catholicism, of Protestant Fundamentalism, of Ethical Idealism, of the Religion of Science, of Liberalism, of Humanism, of New Orthodoxy, and of Agnosticism. The last, which means believing that you cannot be certain of any belief, may be where we will come out after looking at so many differing kinds of faith.

Another area where there is confusion in our time is that of ethics. Here is the side of religion which has to do with how one lives. The mood of modern times was expressed by Walter Lippmann's *A Preface to Morals* which took as its motto the words of Aristophanes, "Whirl Is King." Another book set forth the spirit of our day with the title: *Write Your Own Ten Commandments*. There is a Spanish story about a gypsy who was making confession to the priest. The priest asked if he knew the Ten Commandments. The gypsy replied, "Well, it's this way, I was going to learn them, but I heard talk that they were going to do away with them." In Maxwell Anderson's play, *High Tor*, one of the characters speaks like this: "The very points of the compass grow doubtful these latter years, partly because I'm none too sober, and partly because the great master devil sits on top of the world, stirring up north and south with a long spoon to confuse poor mariners."

Yet another area where there is confusion is that of denominationalism. Here is where we come to the matter of joining a church, but when we start to take that important step we find that there are two hundred and fifty religious groups and sects in the United States of America. Which shall we join? Here is a bewildering array of religious diversity probably unparalleled anywhere else on earth save perhaps in India. To the outsider it must surely seem as if there are two hundred and fifty different answers being given to anybody who wants to know about Christianity. It is a fact that some of these groups do agree with some others on some points, so the confusion is not quite that great, but nevertheless it is not small. As long as this condition continues, it is not to be wondered at if those who are outside are often at a loss as to which church they should join, and end up by not joining any.

Ways Out?

One way by which an attempt is made to escape from this confusion is ecclesiasticism. This is, however, surrender. It is appealing because it means accepting an authoritatively proffered answer, thus escaping the necessity for further inquiry; nevertheless it is unsatisfactory precisely because it involves the abandonment of further autonomous thought. It is akin to the situation where a whole people, burdened by insoluble problems, wearily gives power into the hands of a dictator.

A related and likewise unsatisfactory way out of confusion is biblicism. This is a short cut. Here it is felt that the infallible expression of the will of God is to be found in a single book, every word of which is on the same level of importance. To take this attitude toward the Bible eliminates what should be recognized as the arduous but necessary process of trying to understand how God's revelation has come to man in what is written in this book.

Yet another way is experimentalism. This is a devious and long route which will hardly get us to the goal in time. This method appears to be in line with the spirit of science and thus appeals to many of us on first thought. There is hardly time, however, for each individual to recapitulate all the experience of mankind: to go back and live as prehistoric man, as primitive man, as pagan man, and as all varieties of Christian man; to join all the two hundred and fifty denominations, one after the other, to see which has what we want; to adhere to all philosophies, one after the other; to try all moral codes or to try living without any moral code. There is not time for one person to carry out the entire experimental process all by himself. Actually this is what the entire human race has been doing for thousands and thousands of years. It is the concentrated essence of the understanding that has come out of a specially significant section of that experience, which is handed down through the heritage of the church and embodied in the pages of the Bible. If we want to get very far, we had better take our stand upon the level which has been reached and try to go on from there, rather than go back and attempt to do it all over again in one single life, for which there probably is not time or strength.

A Way

Several positive suggestions may now be made as to how to get out of confusion and on toward confidence and certainty in our Christianity. One suggestion is that we simplify, in the sense of concentrating upon a few central convictions. Everyone has many things about which he is uncertain, but somewhere, deep down within himself, something which he does believe. Let us work back until we find that unshakable thing, and not worry too much if there remain, on the periphery, uncertainties and doubts. The man who is called the father of modern philosophy did this in philosophy. René Descartes, modern in spirit, resolved to doubt everything which he possibly could, and thus he whittled away much that was superfluous with the sharp knife of his skepticism. At last, deep down, he came to something which he could not doubt. Then he began to build upon that. Another man did the same thing in the realm of ethics. Horace Bushnell was an unbelieving tutor at Yale. He prayed: "O God, I believe that there is an eternal difference between right and wrong, and I hereby give myself up to the right and refrain from the wrong." On that simplified foundation of the one thing of which he was convinced, he built further to become one of America's important leaders in religion.

In the story of the healing of the blind man in the ninth chapter of the Gospel according to John, we read how afterward the enemies of Jesus began to pester and badger and persecute the healed man. The latter was evidently a simple-minded man who could not answer all the questions which the shrewd Pharisees flung at him, but at last he made this uncontrovertible reply: "One thing I know, that though I was blind, now I see."[1] As always, the Fourth Gospel is pointing at the universal significance of a specific event. The blind man given sight is a symbol of every Christian. When through contact with Jesus Christ he sees light, that single fact is a sufficient certitude to live by.

A second suggestion is to personalize the matter. This the blind man did. He did not have the answers to everything about which the Pharisees plied him with questions, but he knew Jesus. Many times in life, what we are most sure about is some person. Josephine Amelia Burr wrote:

> I am not sure that the earth is round
> Nor that the sky is really blue.
> The tale of why the apples fall
> May or may not be true.
> I do not know what makes the tides
> Nor what tomorrow's world may do,
> But I have certainty enough
> For I am sure of you.

Think of this in terms of encounter with a great Christian personality. Harry Emerson Fosdick tells of a friend of his who, when a student at Harvard University, went to see Phillips Brooks about a problem. After the conference he was walking home with his head held high and his heart light, when he suddenly realized he had never asked the particular question with which he had gone. He said: "But I did not care. I had discovered that what I needed was not the solution of a special problem but the contagion of a triumphant personality."[2] Then lift this matter on up to the level of a personal encounter with Jesus Christ himself. How often it has been true that to know him, to personalize the matter in terms of loyalty to him, has given not the answers to all technical and theoretical questions, but the central certainty by which man can live. As George Matheson said: "Son of man, whenever I doubt of life, I think of thee."

Finally, it is needful to vitalize the matter. The suggestion here is of the necessity for taking action. In so far as we can see a single step to take, whether that of joining a specific church even though it is admittedly imperfect, or that of doing some deed to which we feel a moral imperative, the step is to be taken, for only by so doing may the way open for the next step beyond.

6. At Ease in Zion

There is a natural longing for ease. When the officer commands, "At ease!" that command at least is received gladly. When Dale Carnegie's book *How to Stop Worrying and Start Living* was advertised under a misprint, *How to Stop Work and Start Living*, many of us were more interested in it than before.

The Church of the Heavenly Rest in New York City is a very beautiful church, but because of its name stories have gathered about it. It is related that a man joined another church in that vicinity. After the minister had welcomed him he said, "We are delighted to receive you into membership in this church. Now where will you work? Would you like to be on the finance committee? Will you work in the men's club? Will you serve as an usher?" The man, somewhat taken aback, replied, "Oh, I do not want to do anything, I just wanted to join the church." The minister said, "I am afraid this is the wrong place; you had better go around the corner and join the Church of the Heavenly Rest!"

There is not only a natural longing for ease; there is also a natural necessity for rest. The Old Testament enunciates the great principle that man shall labor and do all his work in six days and rest on the seventh. Today a man working on a staggered shift will perhaps not be able to keep the Sabbath quite like a Jew of ancient Palestine, but we certainly dispense with this principle of rest only at our own peril. In the New Testament Jesus' gracious invitation is extended: "Come to me, all who labor and are heavy-laden, and I will give you rest."[1] So the Bible recognizes fully the natural necessity for rest.

The Condemnation

But it also contains the word of the prophet Amos: "Woe to those who are at ease in Zion."[2] We will study first the condemnation which is implied in these words. Who are these people concerning whom this condemnation is uttered? They are the people of Jerusalem and Samaria. Zion was another name for Jerusalem. In the second part of the verse there is mention of those who trust in the mountain of Samaria. That was the great hill in northern Israel on which the fortified capital of that land was built. So these are the people of Jerusalem and Samaria. They are the people of the middle of the eighth century B.C. The Book of Amos contains reference to Uzziah, king in Jerusalem, and Jeroboam, king in Samaria. We know something of what conditions were like at that time. Uzziah enjoyed a long and stable reign, during which Judea experienced prosperity. Jeroboam II was particularly

successful in military accomplishment. He won wars
for his people, and northern Israel enjoyed the fruits of
victory; there was prosperity there.

In this situation many of the people of Jerusalem
and Samaria became lazy. Those who are at ease in
Zion are therefore, first of all, the people who are lazy.
Amos' description of it is very vivid when he speaks of
"those who lie upon beds of ivory, and stretch themselves upon their couches, and eat lambs from the flock,
and calves from the midst of the stall; who sing idle
songs to the sound of the harp, and like David invent
for themselves instruments of music; who drink wine
in bowls, and anoint themselves with the finest oils."[3]
The entire picture is evidently that of the enjoyment
of a banquet. It was an ancient oriental custom to
recline to eat. Here at Samaria the couches were
adorned with ivory plaques, beautifully carved. Many
of these ivories have been found in fragmentary condition in the excavation of Samaria. Such was the chief
interest of the people. They were lazy, indolent, and
spent their time in enjoyment of the prosperity that was
theirs.

The Bible is a very honest book. It does not hesitate to tell about these and others who were lazy.
Sometimes men missed out on great hours because of
their laziness. Moses toiled up Mount Sinai to meet
with God. He told his people before he left them,
"Be ready." Instead of keeping themselves in readi-
ness, we read that they "sat down to eat and drink,

and rose up to play."[4] Some of them missed out on participation in the very birthday of the Hebrew nation because of that. Haggai came back and found that the people of Jerusalem had rebuilt their houses after the destruction of war, but had been too indolent to go ahead and get God's house rebuilt. He called them to bestir themselves. A parable of Jesus conveyed a scathing indictment of one man. Described in it, he is called a "wicked and slothful servant."[5] Wickedness and sloth often go together. Jesus left his disciples a little way behind in Gethsemane and went ahead to pray. He came back and had to say to them, "Are you still sleeping and taking your rest?"[6] People have missed great hours because their proclivity for ease and their natural desire for rest have overcome them in great times. These who are at ease in Zion are people who are lazy.

Again, they are people who are complacent about their world. After describing their lounging at their magnificent banquet, idling away their time, Amos says of them: "But [they] are not grieved over the ruin of Joseph."[7] They were callous to the need within their own country. In that day a formula which Communism has popularized would have properly described what was taking place: the rich were getting richer and the poor were getting poorer. These people had no concern for this, however. While they were able to enjoy luxurious ease, they were callous to the need that was about them. Amos was not. Some of the most vivid passages in all literature descriptive of oppression and of great social inequities are those found in his prophecy. But the people who were at ease in Zion were complacent about all of it.

They were also blind to the threat which was coming up from outside. Inside, things were corrupt. Outside, a great threat was approaching. That is an extremely bad combination. When things are corrupt on the inside, then a blow of even moderate force on the outside causes collapse. The time, we have seen, was about the middle of the eighth century B.C., say 750 B.C. In 747 B.C. Tiglath-Pileser became monarch of Assyria and rapidly revived the military power of that land. Within his reign the might of Assyria reached into northern Israel and many captives were taken away. He was succeeded by Shalmaneser. Shalmaneser inaugurated the siege of Samaria. By 721 that city fell to the next Assyrian monarch, Sargon. Within thirty years, then, complete military disaster came upon this complacent people who cared not that within, the moral foundations of the country's life were crumbling, and who saw not that without, a threat was arising of the utmost gravity. They were complacent about their world.

Once again, these whom our prophet describes were satisfied with themselves. In the description of them by Amos we find it said in the King James Version that they "trust in the mountain of Samaria," but in the American Translation that they are "self-confident on the mount of Samaria."[8] They were satisfied with themselves because they were such thoroughly religious people. They brought their sacrifices every morning and their tithes every three days, as Amos says. But Amos tells them what God thinks of it: "I hate, I despise your feasts, and I take no delight in your solemn assemblies."[9] Another slogan of Communism was evidently applicable: "Religion is the opiate of the people." Their very religious observances helped to deaden their sense of the need for doing anything, and thus, satisfied with themselves, they performed their ceremonies day after day and had no worries, when it would have become them to worry greatly.

The Challenge

Here they are then, and here is the prophet's condemnation of them. But let us now try to read the challenge that is implied by the denunciation. For one thing, it is assuredly the challenge of *work*. They were lazy. We are called upon to work. It is possible to rise up even out of indolence and lay hand to a task that needs to be done. There is a challenge about work. It is a great thing to work. Man's body and mind are both made for work. They atrophy when they are not used. They become stronger when they are employed in constructive tasks. Michelangelo used to say, "It is only well with me when my chisel is in my hand." The very fulfillment of life comes by taking up whatever is your tool and using it and doing the task that you can do with God's endowment.

There is a magnificent passage in an Old Testament apocryphal book, the Wisdom of Jesus ben Sirach, about work. It speaks of people who work with their hands as smiths, potters, painters, builders, craftsmen, and men who hold the plow. It says about them:

> All these rely on their hands;
> And each one is skilful in his own work;
> Without them, no city can be inhabited,
> And men will not live in one or go about in it.
> But they are not sought for to advise the people,
> And in the public assembly they do not excel.
> They do not sit on the judge's seat,
> And they do not think about the decision of lawsuits;
> They do not utter instruction or judgment,
> And they are not found using proverbs.
> Yet they support the fabric of the world,
> And their prayer is in the practice of their trade.[10]

Take up the work that you are called to do. Practicing that work is part of prayer. Jesus said, "My Father is working still, and I am working."[11] He worked. In his early life he was busy in the carpenter shop, dignifying the toil of man with the efforts of his hands. In his public ministry he labored more strenuously than ever. There is a challenge here, the challenge of work.

Again there is the challenge of *concern*. The people Amos described were complacent. We are called upon to be concerned. "Concern" is a Biblical word. Paul speaks about the Philippians and rejoices, "Now at length you have revived your concern for me."[12] It is a word which the Quakers particularly have taken up and brought to life. When a Quaker has a concern he is gripped by something which he must do. It was because of a concern that Wilbur Young moved onto a Mississippi cotton plantation, to participate in the life of the sharecroppers, and ultimately to bring to them the benefit of some wider vision. A concern can lead any man to the place where he can do something to make the world better.

Once again we see the challenge of *aspiration*. The people of Amos' day were self-confident and self-satisfied. We are called to aspiration. He who stood up, as Jesus told, and thanked God that he was not as other people, that he was doing everything that God expected him to do, went down unjustified, whereas the other man who beat upon his chest and cried, "God, be merciful to me a sinner,"[13] went down justified, because he desperately wished to be better than he was. In the stately words of Oliver Wendell Holmes, as he read the lesson of "The Chambered Nautilus":

> Build thee more stately mansions, O my soul,
>   As the swift seasons roll!
>   Leave thy low-vaulted past!
> Let each new temple, nobler than the last,
> Shut thee from heaven with a dome more vast,
>   Till thou at length art free,
> Leaving thine outgrown shell by life's unresting sea!

The Call

So the call sounds, and in the church there is an opportunity to answer it. Are you willing to work? If so, you ought to join the church. There is a place for work in the church. Every Christian who follows Jesus—Jesus of the carpenter shop, Jesus of the hurrying days of his ministry—every Christian ought to be a worker. You ought to work. You ought to join the church.

Do you have a concern? Would you like to be not callous to the need that is round about nor blind to the peril that exists in our world? You ought to join the church, because in the church you can manifest a concern for all humanity.

Do you aspire? Would you like to be better than you are now? You ought to join the church. When you join the church, you do not stand up and boast, "Lo, I am perfect; lo, I am better than other men." No, you make it manifest that you desire to be better than you are; that you desire to grow in Christian life with Jesus Christ. Do you aspire? You ought to join the church. Here is the call, and here in the church is the opportunity.

7. They Had a Mind to Work

The Book of Nehemiah centers around one of the great happenings of the Old Testament. The time was 445 B.C. The Jewish people had experienced a long period of disaster and discouragement. A century and a half before, Jerusalem had been destroyed. It was then a subject city in the Chaldean Empire, and when the people refused to pay their taxes the Chaldean king, Nebuchadnezzar, came and punished them, and when they refused a second time he came and punished them severely. The commanding officer of the Babylonian king came into Jerusalem and burned down the Lord's house and the king's house and all of the houses of the city. Then he broke down the wall of the city all round about. In the ancient oriental world the wall was particularly the strength and the pride of a city. Even today the old part of Jerusalem has a great wall around it, and the ancient cities of the Near East were regularly fortified with powerful walls. The walls stood as symbols of the power and dignity of the city. Nebuchadnezzar's commander, then, cast down the wall of Jerusalem and thus left the city in ruins, open to all enemies, utterly defenseless. Most of the people were carried away into exile, and were there for many years. Then little groups of them began to straggle back. They made places for themselves to live in, and after a while at the urging of two of their prophets they rebuilt the temple, though the new structure was not as fine as the former temple had been. But still the walls of the city of Jerusalem were only rubble, and the city was vulnerable to any who might come. And of course the enemies, of whom there were many, made it their effort in diplomacy and in outright violence to restrict any attempt to rebuild those walls. That was the situation when Nehemiah came back in 445 B.C.

The situation was so discouraging and the perils were so many that, although he was interested in the matter of the walls, he did not dare say so at once in public. Instead he rode round the city by night upon a small beast of burden, accompanied by a few friends, to inspect the ruins. Then he began to talk to the people and to encourage them, and with the contagion of his enthusiasm and purpose a new spirit began to manifest itself among them. They resolved to rebuild the walls of Jerusalem, and actually undertook the long-neglected work. Finally, in Nehemiah 4:6, we come upon the great statement: "So we built the wall. . . . For the people had a mind to work."

Transforming Effect of Mental Attitude

In this account, the transforming effect of mental attitude in the doing of work is evident. The mind has great power in relation to the accomplishment of work. As a matter of fact, Professor J. B. Rhine of the Parapsychology Laboratory of Duke University believes that he has demonstrated that the mind has power to influence matter directly, a power to which he gives the name of psychokinesis. The experiment he employed to establish the existence of this power involved dropping small cubes, with spots on their surfaces, on a table and endeavoring by concentration to secure some particular combination of spots, such as seven, for example. After hundreds of thousands of experiments with many different persons serving as subjects, he is convinced that whatever psychokinesis is, it is something that is statistically measurable.

If that is true, it is hardly more remarkable than what is illustrated in the story of Nehemiah—namely, the power of a change of mental attitude to transform an outward situation. This happens in the lives of individual people. One man has told how at the close of the first World War he returned to the University of Vienna to complete a doctorate in law. His heart was not in this work, however; he was there because it was what his family wanted. Actually his own deep interest was in music, but in that he had seemed to fail, having lost a position as piano player in a small music hall. In his dejection he went one day to an old law professor and told him of his disappointments. He expected to be consoled, but instead the professor opened a book in front of him and asked him to copy down a sentence from it. The sentence was the statement by Socrates: "If a man would move the world he must first move himself." In the light of that principle, this man changed his whole program. He knew there was one thing that he really wanted—namely, to become a symphony conductor—and, disregarding every other consideration, he started to work toward it. Today Artur Rodzinski, a world-famous orchestra conductor, recalls the discovery of the principle enunciated by Socrates as marking the turning point in his life.

This happens in whole groups of people. Look again at those people living in the ruins of desolated Jerusalem. Their city walls were rebuilt because first of all a new attitude was built in their minds. Chapter three of the Book of Nehemiah is filled with names, but read with imagination it presents a thrilling picture. These are the names of individual persons who had a mind to work and who joined Nehemiah in the task. Here are a few of them: Eliashib the high priest, and his brethren the priests, built the Sheep Gate. Even priests were not ashamed to soil their hands with everyday toil! Next to Eliashib were the men of Jericho. They did not even live in Jerusalem. They had to come a long distance to join in the work, but they believed in it and they came. The sons of Hassenaah built the Fish Gate. Next to them the Tekoites repaired. Then the splendid record is broken by this notation: "But their nobles did not put their necks to the work of their Lord."[1] Those were some aristocrats who felt themselves too exalted to descend to menial labor. After that we meet Uzziel, of the goldsmiths, and Hananiah, son of one of the apothecaries, who joined in the work. Then there were Malchijah and Hasshub, who repaired the Tower of the Ovens. And next repaired Shallum, the ruler of half the district of Jerusalem, he and his daughters. Here was royalty of a different sort from that exemplified by the Tekoites. Even the princesses worked. So one finds in the chapter the imperishable record of the names of these people whose minds were transformed and who went forth to labor, as a result of which Jerusalem's wall was built.

Characteristics of a Mind Disposed to Work

A mind that is disposed to work is characterized by its unwillingness to recognize that anything is impossible. Santayana, the great philosopher, has said, "The difficult is that which can be done immediately; the impossible that which takes a little longer." American engineers have formulated the motto, "If you have rivers that can't be bridged, we'll bridge them; mountains that can't be tunneled, we'll bore through. We specialize on things the world says we can't do." An American journalist once put it like this: "There are plenty of people to do the possible; you can hire them at forty dollars a month. The prizes are for those who perform the impossible. If a thing can be done, experience and skill can do it; if a thing cannot be done, only faith can do it." Such is the mind that is willing to work and believes nothing to be impossible. The situation in Jerusalem was hopelessly impossible. San-ballat said, in effect, "You feeble Jews, what are you going to do?" Tobiah said, "Go ahead and build your wall and a fox will walk up on it and knock it down." It was a hopelessly impossible situation, but faith was able to accomplish the impossible.

The mind that wills to work is one that sees the part in relation to the whole. The story is well known of the time when Sir Christopher Wren walked unrecognized among the laborers who were building St. Paul's Cathedral in London. When he asked them what they were doing, one replied that he was earning so much a day; another said that he was cutting stone; but the last declared with pride that he was helping build a cathedral! The small task which he had was made great by its relationship to the whole. It was even so with those who carried the stones at Jerusalem: they were building the wall of the holy city.

Again, those who have a mind to work see the major undertaking as so important that minor irritations become unimportant. As long as human beings work together there will be minor irritations. Perhaps even Eliashib, Uzziel, and Malchijah did not always agree. But the Lord's work was too important to be halted over small disagreements.

The mind that thrills to work has a sense of divine partnership. The most profoundly encouraging thing that Nehemiah said to the people of Jerusalem was that the very God of heaven was concerned, and would be with them and prosper them in the undertaking. Thus in the assurance of divine help, they were bold to defy Sanballat and Tobiah, and proceed.

And, as revealed in the New Testament, the mind that wills to work realizes that the character of even hidden work will some day be revealed. Some workmen do shoddy work in places where they think it will not be seen. If they thought it would be brought to light they might do better. Paul says that the work we do for God will be made manifest. Some of us build with gold, some with silver, some with precious stones, wood, hay, or stubble, but every man's work will be made manifest, for the day will declare it, and it will be tested by fire.

Opportunities

Finally, there are many opportunities in the church to have a mind to work. Many different tasks are to be done. An Old Testament writer spoke about how happy he was to be a doorkeeper in the house of the Lord. He thought that it was a greater honor to do that than anything else. No doubt if he lived today he would be an usher! The first to greet strangers at the door of the church, his enthusiasm and friendliness would be contagious.

There is opportunity for personal work. In one church a man came to his minister one day and asked for names that he might go and call on the people and try to interest them in the church. He finished the list much sooner than was expected, and asked for more. For several years now, two hundred people a year have been won and brought into that church through the work of that one man. He says, "I am having a great experience!"

There is the opportunity of stewardship. This also can be handled best by the mind to work, the spirit that counts it a privilege and a joy. As Paul says in writing to the Corinthians about the Macedonians, "They gave according to their means, as I can testify, and beyond their means, of their own free will, begging us earnestly for the favor of taking part in the relief of the saints—and this, not as we expected, but first they gave themselves to the Lord and to us by the will of God."[2] With such a spirit, the possibilities of accomplishment are illimitable.

8. Greater Things Than These

One of the most remarkable sayings of Jesus is recorded in John 14:12: "Truly, truly, I say to you, he who believes in me will also do the works that I do; and greater works than these will he do, because I go to the Father."

The Works of Christ

Jesus Christ himself did great works, and based his claim upon the works which he did. Early in his ministry, messengers came from John the Baptist to ask him if he was really the expected One after all. At first John the Baptist had pointed to Jesus as the One whose coming had long been looked for, but then after being in prison he grew discouraged and sent these messengers to ask the question. The messengers stayed for a time and saw some of the things which Jesus did. Then he sent them back with this message: "Go and tell John what you hear and see: the blind receive their sight and the lame walk, lepers are cleansed and the deaf hear, and the dead are raised up, and the poor have good news preached to them."[1] That was enough—the things he did—for proof of who he was. Then near the end of his life he said: "Believe me that I am in the Father and the Father in me; or else believe me for the sake of the works themselves."[2] He did great works, and he said that people could found their faith upon the things that were done.

That is in line with a typically American way of thinking in philosophy. It was Charles Peirce who first said that to find the truth of an idea we should examine the consequences to which it leads in action. William James caught up that principle and developed his philosophy upon the basis of it, coining the striking phrase, "Truth is the cash value of an idea." Cash in an idea in practice and see what it brings! You can submit the teaching of Jesus and the facts of his life to this characteristic American philosophical test, and they stand that test. In St. Paul's Cathedral in London is the epitaph of the architect, Sir Christopher Wren: "If you seek a monument, look about you." The great cathedral stands as a monument to its builder. The works of Jesus Christ are the monument of his life. He did great works and rested his claim upon what he did.

The Works of the Disciples

Furthermore, Jesus Christ expects his disciples to do greater works than he did. What an amazing expectation that is! At first sight it appears almost contrary to the teachings of Christianity, because it is our belief that once upon a time on this earth there lived a person who was unique, who was the Son of God in a special sense, and who did the works of the Son of God. We can only marvel and wonder at what he was and what he did. Then we come squarely up against this statement that his disciples are to do greater works than he did himself. That is truly amazing. One would expect him to say that his disciples should remember him. As a matter of fact, he did say that, and his words to that effect are often repeated when the communion service is observed. One might perhaps expect Jesus to say the first words of the statement we are studying: "He who believes in me will also do the works that I do." The Christian certainly ought to live up as far as he can to the example of what Jesus was and did. The "imitation of Christ" has often been recommended. This, too, we might comprehend. But the absolutely amazing thing is that he says his disciples are to do greater works than he did.

Amazing as it is, it is also an actuality. The expectation of Jesus was not altogether in vain. Consider his church. In his own lifetime Jesus probably won to following him and to accepting his teaching some hundreds, but scarcely thousands of people, for when on the Day of Pentecost three thousand were converted it was considered to be a great and unparalleled event. After that, as the disciples went out in missionary work, immensely larger numbers of people were won across the years. In 1940 the last volume of the largest modern history of the expansion of Christianity, that by Kenneth S. Latourette, was finished. The last volume covered the 140 years from 1800 to 1940, and the author said that in that period the church had done more and the influence of Christ had been greater on the earth than during any preceding period. In 1950 the churches of the United States achieved a total net gain of 2,950,987 persons, bringing the grand total church membership in the United States of America to 85,705,280. In a year when the population grew 1.67 per cent, church membership increased 3.56 per cent; and 55.9 per cent of the people belonged to the church. In 1953, the *Yearbook of American Churches* reported a gain for the preceding year of 3,604,124 persons or 4.1 per cent, making a total church membership of 92,277,129, or 59 per cent of the population. In this way, as measured by statistics, the disciples have done greater works.

The same situation may be said to prevail in the works of science, especially medical science. Jesus did wonderful things in healing people—miracles were wrought. But it was a comparatively small number of people who were touched by the direct impact of his hands. It has been an immensely larger number that have been touched by his spirit, working to set men's minds free to become scientists and then, especially because of compassion and concern for humanity, to concentrate upon medical science and the healing of men's diseases. Wonderful things have been done, in a sense greater things than Jesus himself did, as his spirit has moved and impelled men in this area.

Again, see the illustration of his words in the history of the world. Jesus expected that his disciples would move ahead. Some religions in the world are based upon the idea of degeneration. They expect that things will get worse and worse. Other philosophies think that everything goes round and round in circles. But Christianity believes in progress: it could not do otherwise when its Founder expected that his disciples would do greater things than he did. Of course, human history is not a straight upward climb; there have been many times of retrogression; but over all the power of Christ in human affairs has been to lead men to go forward.

Consider these steps of God across several recent centuries: In the fifteenth century the great event was discovery—geographic emancipation. The voyage of Columbus took place in 1492. In the sixteenth century the great event was reformation—spiritual emancipation. Luther nailed up his Theses in 1517. In the seventeenth century the great event was invention—mechanical emancipation. That was the century in which the telescope was first used, and then the microscope, and men began to have effective machines with which to study and deal with nature roundabout. In the eighteenth century the great event was democracy—political emancipation. The Declaration of Independence was signed in 1776. In the nineteenth century came abolition—physical emancipation. The Emancipation Proclamation was penned in 1863. And here we are, now, in the twentieth century. Will there yet be in this century some great event that will also mean emancipation for mankind? If the feelings that are deep in the hearts of the common people of the world are any indication, we are called in this century to make some great step forward in regard to how the nations of the earth can live together in peace. At any rate, across many centuries notable steps of progress have been taken, and in them it is not difficult to recognize that the spirit of Christ has been of influence. To illustrate at a single point, we may recall how Dr. Latourette asks why it was that the Europeans displayed such a remarkable energy in their wide explorations; after wondering if it was something that lay in their race, or was derived from their climate, he considers whether it was not, in part at least, a result of the emancipation of spirit and establishment of human confidence which came from the legacy of Jesus?

So when Jesus long ago did great works and then told his disciples that he expected them to do greater things than these, his words were not spoken in vain. His disciples are truly expected to go on to greater things. The amazing expectation of Jesus has become an actuality. It is, therefore, also a challenge to us. His words apply to our own individual lives. A Christian is not supposed to be satisfied with himself as he is. Even the Stoics had a saying: "He that is not getting better is getting worse." We are expected to go on to greater things in our personal lives. As a group of people in the church we are also expected to do greater things than we have ever done before, and never to be satisfied to sit down and rest and fold our hands. There too, I suspect, if we are not getting better we are getting worse. If we are not doing more we are doing less. Life is such that one cannot stand still—one goes either forward or back—and both individuals and churches must constantly be looking forward to greater things.

The Ground for Hopeful Expectation

But let us not fail to note that if Christ expected his disciples to do much, he did much himself to make their greater works possible. According to John's Gospel, Jesus spoke this word on the last evening of his life. After that, however, he did at least three things to make it possible for his great expectation to come to pass.

First, he was crucified. Previously, men had speculated about God and whether or not his nature was love. Afterward they testified to how Jesus Christ walked out to Calvary and laid down his life for the world, and they pointed to that as the supreme proof of the fact of the love of God. According to John 12:32, Jesus said: "And I, when I am lifted up from the earth, will draw all men to myself." The crucifixion released a new power to attract men.

Then, Christ was raised from the dead. Oppressed by death and saddened by loss, men had long asked and wondered whether, if a man die, he would live again? But now the disciples could testify to the fact of the resurrection of Christ.   On the strength of that fact they went out, themselves unafraid to die, and able to bring a message of hope to all men.

Then there is the third thing that he did, and that was that he sent the Spirit.   He said that when he went to the Father he would send the Spirit, the Comforter. On the Day of Pentecost the early Christians had a great experience when a Power more than themselves came into their midst and became a continuing force in their church work.   It was because of all these things that it was possible for the disciples to do their "greater works."

9. The Cost of Things

Jesus once asked, "Which of you, desiring to build a tower, does not first sit down and count the cost, whether he has enough to complete it?"[1]

Everything Costs Something

It is certainly true that everything costs something. These days one does not need a Biblical text to prove that! Jesus spoke particularly about the cost of building a tower. After the great depression one would drive across the midwestern prairies and see looming up above a small town the skeleton tower of a multi-storied building which someone had planned to erect and, having started, had been unable to finish. He had not estimated the cost with sufficient accuracy, nor taken stock well enough of his own resources.

It costs something to build a life. Some people do not carry that task through, either. Starting out with fine plans and blueprints, they execute them partly but when they find how much it costs altogether they abandon them. Later in life they look back and regard their earlier hopes with wistful sadness. It costs something to obtain what we want in life. An old Spanish proverb declares, "God says: Take what you want and pay for it." Everywhere in life there is a balance. In one pan of the scales is what we want; into the other pan we must place the price which brings the scales to equilibrium.

It costs something to be a Christian. That is what Jesus was talking about most specifically. He was telling his disciples that it would cost them something to follow him. Therefore, he advised, they should think about it carefully ahead of time. To emphasize the point he told not only about the man who built the tower but also about another one who was facing a battle. Before going out to meet the enemy he sought information as to how many forces were in the field, in order to see if he had enough strength himself for the conflict. If not, it would be better to send out an embassy and ask for peace instead of starting the war at all. There are formidable opponents arrayed against the follower of Christ. It is necessary to count the cost before beginning to be a disciple, and to ask whether one is willing to put up the kind of battle it is going to take to win the struggle.

Paying Before or After

While it is true that everything costs something, there is a difference in the way people choose to pay the price. Those who are wise plan and pay the price ahead of time. Those who are not wise do not think ahead of time, and they pay the price afterward. Savonarola, the famous Italian preacher who eventually lost his life for his faith, once put it in these words: "Would you rise in the world? You must work while others amuse themselves. Are you desirous of a reputation for courage? You must risk your life. Would you be strong morally and physically? You must resist temptation. All this is paying in advance. Observe the other side of the picture: the bad things are paid for afterwards."

There are illustrations of paying the price ahead of time in every area of life. That is what a man does in gaining his education. It costs a great deal in time, money, and effort. Probably only long afterward does the time come when, as William James once expressed it in a well-known statement, he wakes up some fine morning to discover that he is actually one of the competent ones of his generation in the line of work which he has chosen. He plans, he pays the price ahead of time, and only later does the prize come into his hand.

The same thing has often happened in the realm of literature. At a dinner, conversation once turned to the great writer Thackeray. A woman remarked to Lord Northcliffe, "Thackeray awoke one morning and found himself famous." Northcliffe replied, "When that morning dawned, Thackeray had been writing eight hours a day for fifteen years. The man who wakes up and finds himself famous, madam, has not been asleep."

In the realm of artistic achievement, the remark of Paderewski comes often to mind, "Before I was a master, I was a slave." Although it was self-imposed, the discipline to which he had subjected himself was very rigorous. Thus it is that those who are wise plan ahead of time that which they wish to build, and ahead of time pay much of the price for it. They pay the price cheerfully and patiently because of the distant goal, and at last they see the successful consummation of what they have undertaken.

The other side of the picture is not as pleasant to contemplate, but it is necessary for full comprehension of the matter. In the study of coins one speaks of the front side as the obverse and the back as the reverse. Every truth seems to be something like that. It has a front side and a back side, and one has to look at both sides to see the whole of the truth. Here, then, we must note that there are those who do not think ahead and do not plan ahead, and therefore they pay the price afterward. Rushing forward, they seize what they want only to find that a price, yet to be paid, is attached inexorably to it. Since everything costs something, we do not avoid paying the price even though the reckoning is postponed for a time. A sentence in a biography of Casanova has been widely quoted. Although the character of the subject is sympathetically presented in the biography, at last comes this statement: "You may envy him until he is forty years of age, but you can only pity him for the rest of his life." That man lived into the seventies—how many years which should have been the best of all were years of pitiable experience!

A woman said to one minister that it was all right to do certain things if she could get away with it. He replied that that was a very big "if," because results always register in yourself. He said that he had formerly thought that the Biblical statement, "Be sure your sin will find you out,"² meant "Be sure your sin will be found out," but had decided that it means exactly what it says, namely that it will find *you* out.

So some people count the cost ahead of time, and other people experience the loss afterward. Some people pay the price, and some pay the penalty. Some get results and some get consequences. Those who are wise plan and pay the price ahead of time; those who are not wise do not plan, and pay the price afterward.

A Worth-While Purchase

Finally we may observe that the possession that is truly valuable and worth paying the price for, is the precious possession of the kingdom of heaven. It is hard in life to know what is worth seeking. Many things lure and beckon us. Some of them turn out not to have been worth very much after we get them. Someone has said that it is like a person standing in front of a store window filled with many items of merchandise, where the price tags have all been shifted around. Here is an item that is marked with a very high price but after you buy it you find that it was not worth very much after all. Here is something else that seems to be readily obtainable but is, in fact, extremely precious. Jesus understood what is worth having in life, and he told us that the kingdom of heaven is the truly priceless possession. He was able to recognize what is counterfeit, what is mediocre, and what is of genuinely supreme worth. He said that the kingdom of heaven is like a pearl of great price which, when a merchant finds, he gladly sells all his other pearls in order to obtain. Again he says it is like a treasure hid in a field, which when a man finds he sells everything he has and buys that field in order to secure the treasure it contains.

The kingdom of heaven is the most precious thing that we can have. It means peace of mind. It means that we are right with ourselves, inside ourselves. The kingdom of heaven means peace of soul. It means that we are right with God. He offers us his forgiveness, and when we accept it with repentance and with faith things are right between ourselves and God. The kingdom of heaven means peace in society. It means that things are right between our neighbor and ourselves. Some day, as men live in this way, things will become right among all men everywhere upon earth. This is the priceless possession of the kingdom of heaven, and it is natural enough that we will have to pay something for it. A man has to pay to start in the Christian life. He has to give up his pride. He has to give up what is wrong. He has to give of himself and his substance in Christian work. But what he is paying for is a priceless eternal possession—the kingdom of heaven.

10. The Price of Spiritual Power

In the Gospels it is narrated that when Jesus and three of his disciples came down from the Mount of Transfiguration they found a crowd of people in the center of which were the other nine disciples, together with a father and his son. The boy was very sick. The symptoms which are given in the account are such as would lead us to diagnose the ailment as probably having been epilepsy. The lad was stricken with spasms, would fall upon the ground foaming at the mouth, and lie in a motionless stupor. In accordance with the world view of that time, it was said that he was possessed by a demon. The father explained to Jesus that he had brought the son to the nine disciples and had asked them to heal the boy. They had tried to do so and had failed. You can almost picture the discomfiture and chagrin of the nine as they stand there with their helpless hands. They have tried to perform a task of healing such as they have seen Jesus do, and they have not had sufficient resources to accomplish it. Jesus did heal the poor sick boy; then afterward, in a private place, the nine disciples asked him how it was that they had not been able to do it. Jesus replied, "This kind can come forth by nothing, but by prayer and fasting."[1]

Fasting

Taking up first the part of this answer which is probably the most difficult to reconcile with our thinking today, we note that a part of the price of spiritual power is said to be fasting. Did Jesus teach that men should do without food until they have weakened their bodies and brought themselves to the point of extinction in order that their spirits may be strong? Some teachers have done that. John the Baptist evidently leaned in that direction, for it was said of him that he came neither eating nor drinking. His disciples were taught to fast. The Pharisees of that time practiced fasting regularly. One of them is pictured in the Gospels as standing up in the temple to pray to God, and his prayer included an announcement to God that he fasted twice every week. In the farther Orient, fasting has been widely practiced. The Jaina monks, who are very thoroughgoing in this, reduce their sustenance to a few grains of rice or wheat a day, and ultimately, as they grow older, end their life by complete starvation. Gautama Buddha fasted at one time in his life to the point that the records say that when he folded his hands over his stomach they rested upon his backbone. Such practices have been adhered to by many people in the world.

Is that what Jesus says is necessary if a man wishes to have spiritual power? I think not. Whereas John came neither eating nor drinking, the Son of man came both eating and drinking, and those who criticized the former as possessed by a demon slandered the latter as a gluttonous man and a winebibber. He was asked why it was that his disciples did not fast when those of John and of the Pharisees did. Therefore it must be that when Jesus said that to have spiritual power a man must fast, he was giving a symbolic general statement which means in our language that a man must give up something for God. In some cases it may be felt by a person that it is food which he should give up for the sake of God. Jesus must have meant that whereas not everybody is required to do that particular thing, everybody is called upon to give up something for God, and nobody is really strong before God until he really does sacrifice something for him. I do not want to make this easier than it actually is; but I do want to try to show that it is something which is inevitably necessary in life. So let us take two or three steps toward an understanding of the fundamental principle.

Consider for one thing that the person who wishes to attain physical power and prowess often gives up something in order to do so. Great athletes do not hesitate to make unequivocal statements on this subject. Glen Cunningham, one of the fleetest human beings ever to flash around the race track, has said that he does not believe anybody can work or run up to his real ability if he smokes or drinks. He was not afraid that he would fail to defeat an athlete who smoked or drank because, when the going got tough, that one folded up. Gene Tunney, the famed prize fighter, said that no fighter or athlete in training smokes. That is because he knows that when a supreme effort is demanded of nerves, muscles, heart, and brain, they must be at their very best if he is not to fail. The point is unmistakable that those who wish to obtain special power and prowess physically are willing to give up something in order to do it.

As one reads the lives of great artists in various fields, again and again there is a story of privation, of deprivation, and of sacrifice, in order to gain the ability which is coveted. In intellectual pursuits, the statement of a professor may be recalled who said that he endeavored to teach his students just two things, namely, discrimination and renunciation. Discrimination is telling the difference between things, which are more valuable, which less; and renunciation is giving up what is less worth while in order to get what is more worth while.

Then come on to the matter of spiritual power. Is it not inevitable that in order to have spiritual power, a person must give up something for God? What must we give up? Our sins, assuredly. We must drop them and cast them away. Our money? Some of it, not that it is bad, but that a token may be shown to God that we mean to use all of it as he wishes us to do. Our time? Yes, some of it may be given up in his service. Perhaps it is something of pride, of cantankerousness in disposition, of resentment or bitterness against someone else, that we are called upon to surrender. What it is, each must determine for himself, but everyone must give up something.   It is on the day that we give up something for God, willingly, that we stand up with the greatest spiritual power we ever had.

Prayer

The other prerequisite of power is prayer.   Prayer is necessary for spiritual power.   It is practice in the spiritual life.   Returning again to the comparison with the experience of the artist, we know that he loves that to which he is devoted, music or whatever it may be, and that he wishes to enjoy power in that field.   But he does not attain this result automatically.   He does not obtain this benefit without arduous practice, even though his talent is great.   Paderewski said: "If I go one day without practicing I can tell the difference. If I go two days without touching the piano, my friends notice the difference.   And if I go three days, the audience knows the difference."   Alongside that, set the remark of E. Stanley Jones: "I am better or worse according as I pray more or less."   Or approach the matter from another angle, remembering that prayer is making connections with available power.   I once heard a marine engineer talking about a boat upon which he was working.   The battery, he said, was full of power, but there was such a confused mass of poorly connected, badly insulated wires between the battery and the engine that that power was not getting through, and the engine did not go.   There is power in the universe, God's power.   Prayer is opening the way for that power to become effective in us. Alexis Carrell has called prayer a force which is as real as terrestrial gravity, and the only power in the world which seems to overcome the so-called laws of nature. He says that when we pray we link ourselves with the power which spins the universe.

In *A Preface to Prayer*, Gerald Heard has given an account of the Curé D'Ars, J. B. Vianny, a man who lived into his seventies, who died in 1859. Even as a boy he seemed to have special gifts in prayer. After he was appointed to D'Ars, power began to be manifest in his parish. There were wonderful healings, and money was marvelously forthcoming for charitable purposes. But when these and other events began to transpire, it was after this man had been praying in an empty house with great intensity for several years, had been fasting, keeping long night vigils, and even scourging himself. Surely some of these practices were aside from the intention of Jesus, yet it seems undeniable that the saintly man actually stored up and also spent prodigious amounts of power. He would stay in his church for seventeen hours a day, hearing the troubles of his people, even though it was suffocatingly hot and strong men would leave within a couple of hours, saying they could not stand it any longer. From his hands and from his lips came power to help people in their trouble. Even if we doubt the wisdom of his extreme ways, the reality of the power which worked through this man who both fasted and prayed can hardly be doubted.

What Spiritual Power Does

If we pay the price of praying and of giving up something for God, we may believe that power will be released whereby we may overcome problems by which we might otherwise be defeated. The story has been told of a man who was the vice-president of a wholesale company. He did his work well. He confidently expected that some day he would be president. When the president died, an outsider was brought in and bitterness settled within his heart. He went on working, but what he did was not effective. Then one evening while reading he came upon a simple prayer, and found himself really praying it. It spoke of being gentle in all events, especially in disappointment. It asked for help to use suffering to make one mellow instead of bitter, and patient instead of irritable. The next morning when the man saw the new president he spoke to him in a friendly way without realizing it. The latter recognized the different tone in his voice and invited his help with a problem. Peace came back into that man's heart and stayed there.

Prayer is a power potentially capable of changing not only ourselves but the world. Frank C. Laubach believes that if ten million persons would start praying and continue until their minds were in full accord with the will of God, it would tip the balance for salvation in world affairs. As he affirms, we are not helpless about ourselves, our future, or our world. There is an open way to power.

11. It Is Difficult to Be Different

When Paul said, "Do not be conformed to this world but be transformed by the renewal of your mind,"[1] he spoke of something which is difficult to do.

Conformity Is Easier

It is difficult to be different because it is easier to be conformed to this world. Among the factors which are powerfully at work in the world today, is mechanization. The freedom of craftsmanship which individual workers had in an earlier time largely disappears with mechanization. In Mexico I watched a man dip a long blow tube into a molten mass of glass and then lift it up, blow through the tube, twirling it at the same time, and thus form a tumbler. No two tumblers he made were alike, each was an individual production. But we usually make things by a machine process where each thing turned out is just exactly like the other. The inevitable concomitant of mechanization, therefore, is standardization. If you mechanize you must standardize. Each bolt must be exactly the same length and each piece of metal formed with exactly the same curve. Furthermore, we have stylization, which is the tendency to establish a style and then have it prevail. A high school student would hardly venture out with a pair of shoes which were different from the shoes which all his classmates are wearing, and all the rest of us— men and women also—are influenced by style.

Again there is what we may call habituation. When we do something once we tend to do it the same way again. Thus a groove of habit is readily formed. In our world there is also indoctrination. This means inculcating opinions or ideas so that others will acquiesce in them. And we experience intimidation. This is found not only in a police state, but also to a degree in ordinary society. Many of us do things because we are afraid of what people will say about us if we do not do them. The reason most people begin to drink is doubtless not that what they take tastes good the first time, and certainly not that they anticipate ending up, as a sizable proportion will, as alcoholics, but simply because they are afraid of what other people will say or think.

Now all of these factors work in the direction of producing conformity and uniformity. The mechanization of the world tends to make men like machines. Some years ago a book was published under the title *F. O. B. Detroit.* In it a character named Russ expressed his opinion of machines. He thought that some machines build men up, but that others tear them apart and grind them down. When a man is geared to a machine, he must follow its speed and recognize that it is the real boss.   He becomes only a small mechanical part of a mechanical process.

Standardization and stylization tend to impress the same mold not only upon materials but also upon minds.   A number of years ago when the custom of bobbed hair came in for the first time, somebody asked Jane Addams what she thought about it; with her characteristic wisdom, she replied that she was not too much worried about the uniformity on the outside of people's heads, but she was bothered by the uniformity on the inside.

The factor of habituation leads us to perform the same maneuvers after they have become meaningless. During World War II, I read a story about the Germans who came out to mine the English Channel.   One day they sowed their mines, and the next day the British went out and swept them up.   With methodical German thoroughness, the next day more mines were planted, only to be swept up by the British on the following day.   This continued with unvarying regularity for some time, until one day for some reason or other the British failed to go out and sweep up the mines.   The next day the dependable enemy came right back on schedule and blew up on their own mines! Lest this story seem to be prejudiced on one side of the picture, let me add a second.   It was published in the London *Star*, where it was reported that every evening at 7:45 o'clock the people walking in Aske Gardens in Pitfield Street, Hoxton, were warned that it was closing time.   The caretaker would then go over and shut and lock the gate. The only strange thing about all of this was that there was no fence or wall around the rest of the park, this having been torn down many years before. When the caretaker was asked why it was that he kept on locking the gate, he replied, "I have never been told not to. It seems silly to me, but I shall have to go on doing it until I am told not to."

The result of indoctrination is to make us think alike. Some years ago Sonja Henie appeared on the screen for the first time wearing white skating shoes. In the week that followed, every pair of white skating shoes in the United States was sold. Popeye is credited with a forty per cent increase in the sale of spinach. In view of such facts, the Payne Fund once set twelve psychologists to work for two years to make a serious study of the influence of the movies. They took a large number of young people and asked them what they thought about such things as the Chinese, the Negro, war, crime, and capital punishment. Then they sent them to see movies which dealt with those subjects, and afterward they questioned them again. They found that the majority had swung over to conform with the ideas that were presented in the pictures. Sitting in the darkness, completely relaxed, with attention focused on the brilliant screen, the psychological conditions are well calculated for the process of indoctrination to take place. So we get conformity of ideas.

As for intimidation, when we encounter its perhaps subtle but nevertheless real force, it is much easier to do like the Negro caretaker who said, "I just throw my mind in neutral and go where I'm pushed." So it is difficult to get out of the groove of conformity and uniformity, when such powerful factors in the world are working to make us conform.

It Is Desirable to Be Different

Nevertheless it is desirable to be different. Paul says, "Do not be conformed to this world." I know that I ought to be different from what I am. Long ago Augustine said, "Whatever we are, we are not what we ought to be." Carlyle remarked that "the greatest of faults is to be conscious of none."

We need people who are different from the dead level of mediocrity in the world, and we need people who want to make the world different from what it is now. Omar Khayyam expressed the desire for a re-making of the world when he spoke about grasping "this sorry scheme of things" and shattering it to bits, and then remolding it "nearer to the heart's desire." In view of his total philosophy it seems doubtful if he really believed that this could be done. But Edwin Markham believed it could when he wrote that "we men of earth have here the stuff of Paradise," and declared that we need no other material than what is right here to "build the stairs into the unfulfilled." We need people who believe that and who try to make this world a different place from what it is now. Paul points to that when he says that we should not be conformed to this world as it is.

The Secret of Transformation

Paul not only states the need for transformation, he also suggests the way in which it is to be attained. He says that we must be transformed by the renewing of our minds. In that statement he gives us a plan. Transformation must begin on the inside and from there work to the outside and to the surroundings. An aged man, who had learned a great deal about living, said to a minister that he had come to the point where he prayed for only one thing, namely, that he might be right within himself. He said that he had discovered that if he thought right and was right, then everything would go right. That, he declared, was all that a man needed to ask for.

But is it really possible for a man to become different from what he has been? Consider the story of Edward Wilson. In 1891 he was a student in Cambridge University, called by his fellow-students "Bill the Cynic." He himself admitted how disagreeable he was in character. When he had an altercation with a friend whom he offended, he afterward wrote to him: "I know I am hard, proud, conceited, scornful, bitter and hard and insulting very often, and always selfish; but I don't like you to treat me as though I weren't trying to do a bit better." Is there any chance for a young man like that ever to become different from that? That same man later went with Captain R. F. Scott on his famous expedition to the South Pole. There, where men's tempers wore thin with close association and trying circumstances, Edward Wilson was known as "Bill the Peacemaker." When he and Captain Scott lay dying together in the snows of the Antarctic, Scott wrote a letter in which he said, "If this letter reaches you, Bill and I will have gone out together. We are very near it now; and I should like you to know how splendid he was at the end, everlastingly cheerful and ready to sacrifice himself for others. His eyes have a comfortable blue look of hope, and his mind is peaceful with the satisfaction of his faith in regarding himself as part of the great scheme of the Almighty."

Can the world become any different? Henry P. Van Dusen has told how, a little over a hundred years ago, the first two British Methodist missionaries landed on an outer island of the Fiji archipelago. They found a people unmercifully cruel, whose common practices were polygamy, strangling, infanticide, and cannibalism. War racked the islands constantly. War canoes were launched over the backs of living men. Heathen temples were consecrated by burying men alive. Anybody who was shipwrecked was regarded as condemned by the gods and doomed to die and so was dispatched at once. A century has passed and what is the situation? Of the population of Fiji, 84 per cent are literate, 99 per cent are Christian, and almost 90 per cent are Methodists! The islands enjoy schools, hospitals, a college, and churches. In one of the churches there is a great stone which once was the sacrificial stone in a pagan temple, where helpless victims were dashed to their death. Now it is the baptismal font in the church

—silent symbol of an amazing transformation. Yes, it is possible even for the world to be made over when people commence to be made over by the power of Jesus Christ. Do not be conformed to this world as it is now, because that is not good enough. Be transformed by the renewal of your mind in Jesus Christ.

12. Conscious and Unconscious Religion

For some of us, to live the religious life seems to require a great deal of conscious effort, while for others, religion seems to be such a natural and spontaneous thing that they are almost unconscious of it. In the first place we will try to describe the kind of people who have an unconscious naturalness about their religious life.

Religion That Is Natural

For one thing, they keep the commandments without even trying. The Ten Commandments give us great principles of life. They were written once upon a time on tablets of stone. They are written still in the pages of the Bible. But more than that they are principles that are written into how things really are in the universe. As James Russell Lowell once remarked:

> In vain we call old notions fudge,
>   And bend our conscience to our dealing;
> The Ten Commandments will not budge,
>   And stealing will continue stealing.

In relation to stealing, a man may break the commandment and, I am sure, receive the bitter consequence of breaking it. He may be apprehended and imprisoned, which is bitter. Or he may elude detection outwardly, but never inwardly. He will always know that he has been a thief. I was once in a house just after it had been burglarized. It made a strong impression of what a shameful thing it is when one person thinks he has the right to break into the property of others and take the things which are precious to others and for which they have worked hard and long, to strew them all over the house, and to make off with whatever he wants. The person who does that, even if he is not caught, must surely always know that he has done a very mean thing and that until he changes his ways he is a very mean kind of person.

Then there may be some of us who do not break the commandment, "Thou shalt not steal,"[1] but who have an awfully hard time with ourselves to keep from breaking it. We walk through a department store; and there are all the beautiful and desirable things piled on the counters round about us, and we have a hard time not to reach out and help ourselves to something. We have to struggle with ourselves in order to keep the commandment.

But there are yet other people who keep this commandment without even trying. They do not even think about stealing as they walk through the store, it does not even occur to them. Of these three levels of behavior, which is the highest: the first, where we break the commandment, with bitter consequence; the second, where after a hard struggle with ourselves we manage to keep from breaking it; or the third, where we do not even think about breaking it? Surely there is no doubt but that the third and last represents the highest level of life.

Another thing observable about people who have this unconscious naturalness of religious living, is that they practice their religion in the practice of their trade. In their work every day there is a natural expression of their religion. John Oliver Nelson maintains that it is a mistake to apply the designation "full-time Christian service" only to the work of a minister or a missionary or a religious educator. Those are indeed church vocations of special honor, but every Christian who is a real Christian ought to be in full-time Christian service. He may be a blacksmith or a plumber or a locomotive engineer, and still his work can be an expression of his genuine Christianity. Leslie Weatherhead has remarked that he, as a minister, is said to be engaged in a sacred task, and his shoemaker in a secular task. But actually, he declares, a religious shoemaker, one who puts leather and not cardboard into his shoes and makes an honest contribution to the welfare of men, is truly serving God. He recalls, too, that it was after Jesus had been doing carpentry work for twenty years and had not yet preached a single sermon, that the voice of God called him his beloved Son, in whom he was well pleased.

Again, people who manifest this genuine, unconscious kind of religion, worship God everywhere. Like Shakespeare's men they find

Tongues in trees, books in the running brooks,
Sermons in stones and good in every thing.

They are like Linnaeus, the great Swedish botanist,
from whom the Linnaean system of classification of
plants is derived. One day he watched a blossom unfolding. He said, "I saw God in his glory passing
near me, and bowed my head in worship." Mark well,
we did not say that such people worship God nowhere.
Some, I am afraid, take the principle we are consider-
ing and distort it to that end. They do not worship
God in church, and they also do not worship God when
they are out in the midst of nature. Those of whom
we are speaking worship God in church, and in nature
and see him everywhere.

Again, they pray without ceasing. The New Testament contains an admonition to do this. As a conscious
act it is hardly possible. But as an attitude that has
become so habitual as to be almost unconscious, it is
possible. One's life is directed steadily toward the
great source of our being, in dependence, in adoration,
in trust, and in desire to serve. Such prayer is indeed

. . . the soul's sincere desire, unuttered or expressed,
The motion of a hidden fire that trembles in the breast.
Prayer is the burden of a sigh, the falling of a tear,
The upward glancing of an eye when none but God is near.

And once again, they who have the unconscious
naturalness of genuine religion serve the King without
even being aware of it. In a great parable in the

twenty-fifth chapter of the Gospel according to Matthew, Jesus tells about the last judgment when the Son of man calls all people before him and separates them, the sheep on the right hand and the goats on the left. Then he says to those on his right hand, "I was hungry and you gave me food, I was thirsty and you gave me drink, I was a stranger and you welcomed me, I was naked and you clothed me, I was sick and you visited me, I was in prison and you came to me."[2] The most striking thing in the story is the surprise of the righteous when the King says this to them. "Lord," they cry, "when did we see thee?" They did not know they had done it to him. They had simply seen a hungry man and given him food, seen a person in need and responded in the way they felt moved to do. Their experience was like that of the hospitable people mentioned in Hebrews, who entertained angels unawares.

They were like the hero of Tolstoy's well-known story, *Where Love Is, There God Is Also*. This man was a shoemaker, and his shop was on a lower level beside the street, so that his window allowed him to see only the shoes of the people as they went past. Many he could recognize from their boots alone, because he had worked on those boots. One night he had a dream in which it seemed as if his Lord said, "Tomorrow I am coming." So all the next day he looked and watched for his Lord to come. But he never saw him. He did see an old man out in the bitter cold trying to shovel away the snow, and he called him in and gave him a cup of hot tea. He saw a poor woman with a child and, feeling sorry for them in their abject need, he found an old coat and gave to them. He saw a woman selling apples and a boy who snatched one and tried to run away, and understanding the plight of both he tried to reconcile them. That was all he saw, and he was always looking over the shoulders of these people, wondering if his Lord was about to come. At nightfall he was disappointed because the Lord had not come. Then he took up his Bible to read, as he always did at night, and it fell open to a new place, the twenty-fifth chapter of Matthew. When he read the words about those who had served the King by serving their fellow-men, he understood at last that his dream had not deceived him, and that the Savior had really come to him that day.

The Pre-eminence of Such Religion

Now let us notice some of the advantages of this kind of natural, almost unconscious living of the Christian life. Such religion is more genuine and less forced than any other kind. It is not something which is put on on the surface, but it is the way we really are. In the Taoist scriptures of China is this statement:

> The superior virtue is not conscious of itself as virtue;
> Therefore it has virtue.

If religion is like this, then it is less grim and more gracious. It is sometimes the case that we have to struggle very hard with ourselves about something and then, having won a victory over temptation, we are very harsh with someone else who does not win. But this kind of religion will be more gracious and kindly to others.

With this kind of religion we will not be so much at a loss if we are caught out without the rule book, and if we have to handle an emergency situation. If our religion consists in always looking up the rule and then making a terrific effort to apply it, we are in a bad situation if we confront an unexpected dilemma and do not have our book of rules at hand. There is an amazing abandon, almost an unconcern, about what may happen, in the teaching of Jesus. Do you remember what he said to those disciples as he sent them out? "When they deliver you up, do not be anxious how you are to speak or what you are to say; for what you are to say will be given to you in that hour."[3] Such is the promise, and those who trust in it are relieved of much worry ahead of time.

Again, with this kind of religion we are less split into two selves and more living as whole persons. In this kind of religious living there is less bifurcation between Sunday and the week days. There is less opportunity for the poet to make his jibe:

> Their worship's over, God returns to heaven
> And stays there till next Sunday at eleven.

There is less difference between our private life and our professional life. There is less difference, indeed ideally there is no difference at all, between the sacred and the secular. Leslie Weatherhead has a sermon on the question, "Did Jesus Distinguish Between the Sacred and the Secular?" In it he says: "Do not let us talk or think or act as though religious talk and religious exercises were the whole of religion. Let the sleeping love of God breathe a fragrance through every part of our lives, and if the word 'fragrance' seems sentimental, let us substitute 'honesty' or 'industry,' or the words which express that which we lack. Some religious people would do well to remember that religion includes filling out correctly their income-tax form and giving their employer an hour's devoted service of their very best quality for every hour for which he pays. And do not let us think we go out of God's world when we enjoy ourselves; and do not let us think of God as an amiable, absentee Ruler, remote from human life, but as the immanent, creative, loving, personal Force that has made the universe one and can bring harmony into our distracted lives."[4]

Encouragement

Finally let us speak a word of encouragement, for we need to be encouraged in this matter rather than discouraged. As we look at some of the people who seem to be such spontaneous, wonderful, natural Christians, we may feel that we will never come to such a point. But after all, just because there are these different levels of religious living, we may look up from whatever point we have reached, to the next level to which we would aspire.   Even if we are down at that lowest level of suffering the bitter consequences of having broken God's commandments, even at that place we may look up with hope and encouragement, for precisely there is the point of the beginning of repentance and of turning to God.   If we are at the level of having to struggle with ourselves to win victories over some of our temptations and problems, let us with good courage keep up the struggle, remembering that with every victory won we are a step farther advanced toward our goal.   With our very practicing of the principles of Christianity, they become constantly more a part of ourselves, and we may hope some time to have some of that proficiency and that naturalness in Christian living that the great saints have had who have spontaneously shown forth the character of God and the way of Christ.

When we see a great artist perform, it seems so natural, and it seems that he does everything spontaneously, beautifully, and perfectly.   But when we think about it, we realize that this man not only has a natural gift but has also practiced for hours and years in order to attain his mastery.   When we see a great athlete perform, his actions seem the most natural possible.   Watch a tennis player upon the court, and see how his strokes are executed with the minimum of effort and the maximum of effectiveness.   It looks so natural and so simple that you think you can step out there and do it the first time.   But if you try it you find that it is not as easy as it looks.   You cannot do it until you, too, have learned and have practiced for a long time. So sometimes in life this natural, spontaneous, magnificent performance is actually a result of long practice and long endeavor.

Let us, therefore, not be discouraged if we do not always automatically show ourselves to be the best kind of Christians and feel ashamed of ourselves afterward. Even if we suffer the penalty of sin, let us take it as God's call to turn back to him. And if we have to try and try again with ourselves, let us believe that this is the way in which God will shape our spirits and make them such as will some day show forth naturally and therefore happily the indwelling spirit of the Lord Jesus Christ.

13. The Inner Sources of Strength

In the Fourth Gospel it is related that on a journey through Samaria Jesus once stopped at Jacob's well. The disciples went into the village of Sychar to buy food, and in the meantime a woman came out to the well and Jesus talked with her about the water of life. When the disciples returned and offered the food which they had brought, Jesus said, "I have food to eat of which you do not know."[1] This story has a known geographical setting. Jacob's well is still in existence and still in use at the foot of Mount Gerizim, the mountain on which the Samaritan people worshiped then and their descendants worship now. The village of Sychar, from which the Samaritan woman came, is also still to be found on the slope of Mount Ebal across the valley. With the persistence of names in the Near East, it is still called Askar. The story also sets forth something which is indubitably true: that Jesus had inner, invisible, and intangible resources and sources of strength, of which even his closest disciples were not fully aware. It seems probable that Jesus was a strong man physically, since he grew up in the work of the carpenter shop, and lived a strenuous life in his ministry. But beyond the physical strength which he had was certainly an inner strength which was something more than physical.

Indeed, in almost every area of life one finds how man depends not just upon that which can be measured outwardly, but also upon that which is intangible and inner. In the realm of prize fighters, weight is carefully considered, and measurements of biceps, yet that does not always tell the story. Spirit as well as size enters into the picture. It is said that one time two famous fighters, Primo Carnera who had much bulk, and Max Baer who had an irrepressible wit, swung at each other. Both missed, both fell flat to the floor, and both lay there in that ignominious position looking at each other. Then Baer called, "The last one up is a sissy!"

From Whence Strength Comes

Let us endeavor to set down a number of generalized statements about these inner sources of strength. For one thing, we are stronger when we think we are. A neurologist in Great Britain reported upon an experiment with three soldiers during the first World War. The test he devised was intended to measure the effect of their mental attitude upon their physical strength, the latter being registered by a gripping machine. Under ordinary circumstances the average right-hand grip of the three men was 101 pounds. When they were placed under hypnosis, however, and told that they were weak, the strength of their grip fell off and their average was only 29 pounds. When they were told that they were strong, their strength returned to its original average and then climbed beyond that to 142 pounds. They were actually 70 per cent weaker when they believed they were weak, and 40 per cent stronger when they believed they were strong.

Again, we are stronger when we have hope. Fear cripples. Hope strengthens. In the study of primitive religion we find how primitive people practice witchcraft, and how terribly effective it is, although we ourselves can see that it is actually nothing at all. But a man believes that a spell is being worked against him. Perhaps an effigy has been made of him and is being washed away little by little in the edge of the river. Although nothing physical touches him, he weakens and, as I have heard on the island of Sumatra, for example, dies. Over against that, the attitude of hope brings strength to people. A doctor tells about two patients who were examined on the same day. One of them was declared seriously ill and little hope was held out for his recovery. The other was found to have nothing gravely wrong with him and it was expected that he would recover soon. The two diagnoses were written out and placed in envelopes, but by an error the envelopes were reversed. The man who had little wrong with him was told that he was so critically ill that he could hardly expect to recover, and the one who was very ill was given a diagnosis of a slight ailment and a promise of speedy return to health. The man who was hopelessly ill recovered; the man who had little the matter with him died. He died of fear, just as the natives do out there on the island of Sumatra. When we have hope we are stronger.

A person is stronger when he is trying to help someone else. "Nothing makes one feel so strong as a call for help," says George MacDonald. Not long ago, off the Golden Gate, the call for help came from out fog-bound waters. John Napoli, an Italian fisherman of San Francisco, was coming in from the fishing banks, and with an incredible strength hauled into his boat, the rail of which is three feet above the water, fifty-four people who were otherwise hopelessly drowning, each one a dead weight.

We are stronger when we are answering the call of duty. A doctor or a nurse may finish a routine period of service and be very weary. Let an emergency transpire, and weariness is forgotten. The nurse or the doctor returns to the task and continues for many hours.

We are stronger when we are doing a great work. A French archeologist, Henri LeClercq, was the editor of a great French dictionary of early Christian archeology, upon which all of us who make studies in that field depend heavily. It is an encyclopedic work of many volumes, and most of the articles were written by this one man. For more than forty years he pored over manuscripts and sources in the British Museum and continued the researches which are embodied and worthily enshrined in the great work. Once he said to some friends, "They say I will never live to write the end but I reply, 'I have a contract with le Bon Dieu to let me finish volume Z.'" Henri LeClercq died shortly after his publishers in Paris acknowledged receipt of the last page of his manuscript. We are stronger when we are doing a great work.

We are stronger when we are obeying the will of God. Jesus said to his disciples, "I have food to eat, of which you do not know." He said, "My food is to do the will of him who sent me, and to accomplish his work."[2]

Underlying Explanations

How can we explain this fact, so many illustrations of which we have been observing? There is, for one thing, a physiological explanation. The human body is so made that it has special reserves and resources packed away within it which become available in an emergency. The adrenal gland, for example, is part of the physiological equipment of both man and animals. The adrenal gland can pour forth a potent drug known as epinephrin. When a wild animal is startled, this gland goes into play, and the animal leaps away with speed that it could not otherwise attain. Too much of the same drug, of course, can paralyze a person with fear. But fundamentally it provides a person with a special resource in time of emergency.

The explanation is also theological. It is a fact that God has made it so that we will never be up against anything that is altogether too big for us. It is stated in the New Testament that we will never be tempted above our ability, but that there will be a way provided to escape from that temptation. This does not say that God will always put his hand upon us and push us right down that open way, but he will provide it; it will be there if we will look for it. In every testing time it will be possible, in God's plan and purpose, for us to meet the test. Speaking about the whole world and the testing time which we now confront, with such great powers coming into our hands which we must learn to control, Leslie Weatherhead declares that man has never been permitted to make a discovery until he was at the same time brought at least within sight of a means by which to cope with that discovery. If there is a task to be done, God makes it possible for us to do the task. He does not do it for us, but he makes it possible for us to do it. One person still remembers that his college president said to the class on the day of their graduation: "God will never send you into the forest to fell the trees with a penknife. When he gives you new work which you have never done, he will give you new strength, which you have never had." It belongs to the nature of God and of his way of dealing with us, that in temptation and test and task he will give us sufficient strength.

There is also a Christological explanation. This may be perceived in the fact that Jesus Christ was wholly one of us in his life here upon earth, and therefore whatever was real in his life is also at least possible in our lives. It may not be apprehended, it may not be claimed by all of us, but it is at least possible, because he wholly and truly lived a human life among us.

Effective Applications

And now we turn to the application of this matter. As has already been intimated, the first application lies in the emergency. We dare to face the coming of emergencies with the assurance that when they come, extra power and unsuspected resource will be released within us and we will rise to greater heights to meet the need.

Dr. Eric Carlson of the Neurological Institute in New York City was once himself a spastic boy, with that kind of damage in some portions of the brain that made it harder for him to cross the street and put a letter in the mailbox on the other side than for an average person to walk a tightrope over Niagara Falls. His mother, a seamstress, helped him, hour after hour, practicing to move a single finger, for example, as the brain gave its command, until he began to gain some control. One day he was hobbling down the street on his crutches, when a team of horses ran away and headed straight for him. He dropped his crutches and ran a block without realizing what he was doing. That made him know that there were unrealized reserves within himself, and he set out with renewed determination to claim and use them. When he was twenty his mother died and he had to go ahead by himself, but he kept on and eventually such mastery became his that he is now a great teacher of others who face the same problem. He says that concentration on some definite purpose is an incredible source of power.

Another application of our principle is in everyday life. If a wonderful accomplishment like that just referred to can be made by a handicapped man, what would not be possible if the same degree of concentration were applied by a person in the enjoyment of his full faculties? There would be virtually no limit to what could be done.

And the last application which we will mention has to do with eternity. By no human means can we bring the strength and resources of the human body to such a pitch that it can be everlasting. But by concentrating upon the inner relationships to God, we can bring the soul to the point where by his grace—even when death marks the end for the body—the soul itself, the inner center of strength, will be sustained unto everlasting life.

14. Wait on the Lord

Our age is accustomed not to wait but to hurry. It is reported that a woman was very angry when she missed one wing of a revolving door. We may not know what to do when we get there, but we hurry in order to arrive. Some time ago a minister wrote a book under the title, *The Impatience of a Parson*. There are many impatient people in our day. In such a time of hurrying, the admonition of the ancient psalmist, "Wait on the Lord,"[1] may be unfamiliar but at the same time more important than ever.

The Harm of Hurrying

There are many times when we do more harm than good by not waiting. In the thirteenth chapter of 1 Samuel, there is an interesting if somewhat enigmatic story about King Saul, and about a rather foolish thing which he did. He was king and trusted leader of Israel; it was a critical juncture in national history. The Philistines were marshaling their forces to attack Israel. The enemy was reported to have 30,000 chariots, 6,000 horsemen, and "troops like the sand on the seashore in multitude."[2] The children of Israel were frightened. It is said that they hid themselves in caves, in thickets, in rocks, in high places, and in pits. Saul himself was in Gilgal, and the people who were with him are said to have "followed him trembling."[3] Now the king had been instructed to wait for seven days until Samuel, the prophet and priest, arrived and offered sacrifice, then go ahead into the conflict. Saul waited seven days, and Samuel did not come, so he went ahead and made the offering himself, arrogating to himself the position of a prophet and a priest. He had no sooner done so than Samuel came. Saul had a guilty feeling about what he had done, as is evident in his words when he explained that he had "forced"[4] himself. Samuel said that he had been foolish and that his kingdom would not continue. This story may seem to us to give an insufficient ground to account for the downfall of Saul's kingdom, yet at the same time it does seem to point to certain of the weaknesses in the character of Saul which led to his fall and the downfall of his rule. He acted hastily; he could not bear to wait another minute; and his hasty action was one which turned out to be unwise. It is often true that when we act in a hurry, we act in a way that brings us into trouble.

In Saul's action we seem to detect also a note of anxiety and of fear. He went ahead and did what he did out of a sense of panic. When we act in a panic, we usually make mistakes. When we act out of a sense of worry, we are likely to act wrongly and unwisely. We also see that Saul probably acted in a burst of anger. He was wrathful against this prophet of his who had not arrived on time. He did not stop to think that Samuel had a long way to come, and that unforeseen circumstances could have interfered to keep him from getting there punctually, and in his indignation Saul proceeded and performed the sacrifice. When we do something in a flurry of anger, we very often do what ought not to be done. As one looks back upon life, how often the worst mistakes that have been made are those that were made when one acted in a hurry, or out of a sense of worry, or in a flurry of anger. We do not do things wisely, we do not do them well, when we do them in haste, when we do them in fear, or when we do them in wrath. If we would only wait on the Lord, we would avoid many such errors. When we wait on the Lord, our fears have time to subside, our wrath is dissipated, and at last the appropriate time for action comes. Then with the right spirit, and at the right time, we can go ahead boldly and well. As is stated in Isaiah 28:16, "He who believes will not be in haste."

When to Wait

In what circumstances is it appropriate to wait on the Lord? There are so many of these that I shall not hesitate to list a rather long series of them with only brief comments. It is usually appropriate and desirable to wait for the morning. In the darkness of the night, the current of life ebbs and in wakeful watchfulness we are prone to make mistakes in our thinking. If we wait until morning, the light is bright and the day is new, and we can make our decisions in a better way. One man says that he has saved several people from suicide by extracting from them the promise that they would not perform the act until the next morning after breakfast. At that time the whole matter looked different to them. It is a good thing to wait for the morning.

It is a good thing to wait for the noontime. Young people are often in a hurry to get along with life. They cannot wait to grow up. Older people often look back and think that it was very nice to be young, and that it would have been desirable to enjoy those days more fully without rushing unduly to get on into the later parts of life. Indeed, young people sometimes try to crowd into the early morning hours of life all of the experiences which properly belong in the fuller unfolding of life, and in trying to do so they sometimes find that all turns bitter. A young woman only twenty-one years of age left this note: "I am twenty-one. I have seen everything. I know everything. I don't like life. It is cheap; dirty, disappointing. I have had all I want of it." And leaving those words behind, she ended her life. It is better to wait on the Lord, so that life may proceed in accordance with its natural sequence and normal unfolding. There will be time enough for everything.

It is a good thing to wait for the evening. Epictetus, who was a lame slave under the Emperor Nero—not a very enviable position on any ground—but who at the same time was a great philosopher, wrote these words: "My friends, wait for God! Wait till he gives the signal and releases you from this service, then go to him. For the present, be content to remain at the post where he has placed you. . . . What else can I, a lame old man do, but sing hymns to God? . . . Since I am a reasonable creature, it is my duty to praise God. Nor will I ever desert this post as long as it is vouchsafed me; and I exhort you to join me in the same song."

It is a good thing if we can wait on the Lord, being patient behind closed doors. Sometimes the doors seem to swing shut, and we have to wait a long time, but that waiting may be necessary and important. Paul was always eagerly looking forward to the next tasks, the next places where he wanted to go, yet again and again imprisonment stopped him. We know that he was in prison for two years at Caesarea, for two years more at Rome, and probably for other periods at several other places. Yet out of Paul's imprisonments came some of his deepest thought and some of his greatest letters. Nehru of India, a man of destiny in the Orient, spent many years in prison. Out of those prison years came some of his great writing and doubtless some of his wisdom and insight. Someone tells of being in the study of George Miller. While there he turned through his Bible and came to that verse in the Psalms which says, "The steps of a good man are ordered of the Lord."[5] He noticed that Miller had written in the margin, "And the stops, too." Sometimes the stops are as valuable as the steps.

Wait on the Lord for a clear channel and a plain road by which to go ahead. During the rule of Saul there was another man who was better fitted to rule

Israel than he. That was David. There were many indications that he was to become king, but he so respected Saul as the anointed of the Lord that he restrained his own hand. He took no step whatsoever against Saul until the day of his death. Only after the death of Saul in battle was the path open for David, and then he stepped forward to become Israel's greatest king, the one to whom they looked back ever afterward with the utmost of admiration.

Wait for the harvest. Jesus told a parable about the seed which grows secretly. Sometimes the best you can do is to plant a seed, and then trust in the great forces which will bring to fruition that which has been planted. By anxiety, by forcing, by pushing, you cannot do anything to help—perhaps only to harm. Wait for the harvest.

"Wait on the Lord," wrote the psalmist, "be of good courage, and he shall strengthen thine heart: wait, I say, on the Lord."

How to Wait

What must one learn if one would live in this way of waiting on the Lord, instead of rushing ahead in hurry and worry? It is obvious that we must learn to pause. Some years ago, when the hurrying spirit of our time was becoming evident, James Truslow Adams said: "Perhaps it would be a good idea, fantastic as it sounds, to muffle every telephone, stop every motor and halt all activity for an hour some day, to give people a chance to ponder for a few minutes on what it is all about, why they are living, and what they really want." It is hardly probable that such an hour's cessation of general activity will ever take place, but each of us can practice the principle involved for himself. Each one of us can learn to pause, if not for an hour, at least for a moment. Sometimes even a moment is enough for things to straighten themselves out. Some groups of businessmen are learning the value of "idea sessions" and are deliberately spending time in silence waiting for ideas to come into their minds. They find that when they do this, not only new ideas come into their minds, but also new feelings of confidence and power.

Learn to pray. To pray is to wait on the Lord. It is clear that the word of the psalmist contains a twofold suggestion. We have to wait for the Lord that things may be worked out in his good purpose which we cannot accomplish by our foolish, feverish hurrying forward. And as we wait for the Lord we wait on the Lord, confident that he is, that his purposes are greater than ours, and that in his own good time he will bring that to pass which is in accord with his will and with our deep desire, when it is right with him.

Learn to have patience. "Let patience have her perfect work."[6] One person recalls how often she heard those words quoted to her as she was growing up. It was her grandmother who had said them to her repeatedly. The grandmother became deaf at twenty-two, yet reared four children successfully. The granddaughter became a writer and later said, remembering the teaching received in her youth, that whether it was painting a more beautiful picture, molding a lovelier daughter, building a lasting marriage, or bringing peace to the world, "someone's patience must temper the work."

Learn to persevere. Persevering in our present task is a part of waiting on the Lord. Jacob Riis, who did so much to better slum conditions in this country, who waged such a long hard battle for that great end, used to get discouraged. He said that when he was tempted to discouragement, he would go down to where a stone-cutter was at work, and would watch him strike blow after blow upon the hard unyielding stone. The man might strike the rock as many as one hundred times without making a crack in it, and then at the one hundred first blow it would split in two. It was not that single blow which did it, however, but all that had gone before. As we wait for the Lord to bring to reality what we desire so deeply and earnestly, let us persevere in the striking of the blows that are given us to strike, waiting upon him as we pause in the hurry of life, as we send our prayers to him, as we seek to possess our hearts in patience. Thus we may wait confidently, believing that he will bring to pass all things that are good.

15. Responsibility, Ltd.

Business companies pay attention to the definition of their responsibilities and liabilities. The liability of their shareholders is also often limited and this is indicated by the abbreviation "Ltd." after the company name, or, in Germany, by the four letters, G. m. b. H., standing for *Gesellschaft mit beschränkter Haftung*, or Society with Limited Liability. Once I was waiting for a ship at Port Saïd. In the interim I occupied myself with reading the printed matter on the back of the steamship ticket. By the time I had finished, I was not certain whether it would be wise to board the ship when it came or not. The printed matter on the back of the ticket was concerned with telling all the things which might happen, and with making it plain that the company would have no responsibility if they did take place. Among eventualities which were in prospect (according to these paragraphs of tightly packed reading matter) were mutiny of the crew, incompetency of the captain, piracy on the high seas, hurricane, iceberg, and many other kinds and varieties of marine cataclysm and disaster. The company apparently did not even think it very probable that the ship would go to the port for which I had bought a ticket, and explained that in that case it was not their responsibility either. Even if the ship did proceed to the destination, it was explained that it might just anchor out at sea and not tie up at a dock at all, and again they were not responsible. So I pictured myself mournfully abandoning my luggage, committing myself to a floating plank, and hoping to drift ashore at my destination. After I read these materials, I decided that they really needed the term "Ltd." after their title. They were a company of limited liability, almost of utter irresponsibility, for the furtherance—or hindrance—of travel!

More recently I have been reading the insurance policy on a boat. This starts out in a very inclusive way. In the quaint language of immemorial seafaring custom, it states:

> Touching the adventures and perils which we, the assurers, are contented to bear, and do take upon us, they are of the seas, men-of-war, fire, enemies, pirates, rovers, assailing thieves, jettisons, letters of mart and countermart, reprisals, takings at sea, arrests, restraints and detainments of all kings, princes and people of what nation, condition or quality soever, barratry of the master and mariners, and of all other like perils, losses and misfortunes that have or shall come to the hurt, detriment or damage of said yacht or any part thereof.

This sounds very good. But pasted onto the policy a little farther down is a statement which declares that in the case of the only one of the aforementioned eventualities that is really likely to happen, namely, war together with the use of weapons employing atomic fission or radioactive force, the assurers will have no responsibility whatsoever. As someone says: "The large print giveth, and the small print taketh away!"

Now let us turn to a serious consideration of the general subject of responsibility. For what are Christians responsible and for what are they not responsible? What are the outlines of Christian responsibility?

Perils

Note first the perils which exist on either side of a right Christian responsibility. On the one side there is the peril of irresponsibility. Some of us are not willing to take responsibility for anything. This irresponsibility is conscienceless. Near the beginning of the Old Testament is the story of the first murder. Cain slays Abel, his brother. Then God speaks to him, doubtless through the voice of his conscience. The Lord God says to Cain, "Where is Abel your brother?" It is the voice of conscienceless irresponsibility which speaks as Cain replies, "I do not know; am I my brother's keeper?"[1] Irresponsibility is callous. In the New Testament is the story of the Good Samaritan. There is the man who was fallen upon by robbers, robbed, beaten, and left lying upon the road. Along comes a priest, who looks at him, and draws his robes closer about him and passes by on the other side. Along comes a Levite and looks at the poor man, and goes by on the other side. This is the callousness of irresponsibility which is unwilling to recognize that a man who is near and in need is one's neighbor and one's responsibility.

Irresponsibility lacks a corporate sense. E. Stanley Jones once told about being in a city in China which was very dirty. A Chinese gentleman said that the encyclopedia called it the dirtiest city in the whole world. Dr. Jones said to his Chinese friend that he did not understand it: the shops and stores were beautiful and clean, and the Chinese gentlemen in them were dressed in silk; but the narrow streets were filthy. In reply the other man pointed out that it was easy to understand, because the shops and stores belonged to their proprietors, but the streets did not belong to anybody. Dr. Jones commented that they all wallowed in corporate filth because of a lack of corporate responsibility.

Being conscienceless, callous, and lacking in corporate sense, irresponsibility is certainly unchristian. That is on one side. But there is also a peril on the other side. This is the peril of over-responsibility. Some of us take responsibility for everything, and when we do, we sometimes get ourselves in trouble. We become meddlesome by doing it, looking after other people's affairs more than after our own. Consider Peter in the story which is told about him in the twenty-first chapter of the Gospel according to John. Jesus cancels out Peter's threefold denial by asking three times if he loves him, and Peter declares his love three times over. Jesus then commissions him in thrice-repeated words to feed his lambs and his sheep. After that he speaks a word about how, when Peter was young, he walked where he wanted to, but when he is old, he will be bound and led where he does not want to go, this being a veiled statement of the martyrdom with which Peter's life was to end.   Then there comes another disciple, the one who is called in the Fourth Gospel "the disciple whom Jesus loved."   Now Peter commences to think about him.   "Lord," he asks, "what shall this man do?"   Jesus, evidently seeing in Peter more of a disposition to meddle in the affairs of another man than to work at his own task, speaks to him and says, "If I will that he tarry till I come, what is that to thee? follow thou me."[2]

Over-responsibility is sometimes mischievous.   Here is a description in a later letter of the New Testament of some people who were in the church at that time: "Besides that, they learn to be idlers, gadding about from house to house, and not only idlers but gossips and busybodies, saying what they should not."[3]   These are people who think that everybody's business is their business, and go putting their fingers into it, and this meddlesome, mischievous maliciousness shows us how wrong over-responsibility can be.

Over-responsibility also tends to be morbid.   People have a sense of guilt for doing wrong, and that is something which is intended to help us get straightened out to go in the direction of what is right.   But with over-responsibility sometimes comes a morbid sense of guilt for everything.   A recent article in the *New York Times* Book Review Section was discussing present-day literature in Germany, and stated that it was characterized by such a morbidity as this. Dostoyevsky's doctrine that "everyone is guilty toward everyone else for everything that happens" was regarded as oppressing the literature of the present time there.

Right Responsibility

Now let us see if we can mark out some of the lines of right Christian responsibility. First, we are responsible for the character of our own discipleship, rather than for decrying that of someone else. Here is Peter. His responsibility is to follow Christ, not to be worried about what John does, and he must concentrate upon that, because that is his main responsibility. Jesus once warned his disciples that it was easier to see a mote in their brother's eye than a beam in their own. We can always discern the fault in somebody else and be oblivious to the same thing on a larger scale in ourselves. We are sometimes suspicious of other people, that they will do something, without realizing that that same thing may be the great temptation to which we will fall prey some day. We must concentrate upon the character of our own discipleship without being too critically concerned about other people.

It is our responsibility to make the church worthy to lead, rather than to scold people who do not follow. We have endeavored in these days to cry to the nations that they should unite, but it has been a still-divided church which has been saying this, and it behooves us to find a greater Christian unity so that what we say as we call upon others to join together will be impressive and convincing.

It is our responsibility to concentrate upon Christianizing the social order where we live, and then it will be possible to speak about where other people live. A Southern Baptist minister in Jonesboro, Louisiana, once preached a courageous sermon on "Overturning Some Tables in the South." He told about how a group of students at an eastern divinity school once went to picket a theater where a certain moving picture about the South seemed to embody racial prejudice. He noted, however, that the students walked past several hotels and restaurants in their own city which did not serve Negro people, when they went to picket the theater. He remarked that it seemed almost ironical that they would hasten to denounce southern folklore and fail to notice the cancers within their own society. Then he went on to urge his own people to be careful lest they make the same mistake. He felt that it was not their business to tell New York how to overcome its discrimination against the Jew, a problem which New York itself must solve; nor to tell California how to overcome its discrimination against the Japanese, a problem for which California is responsible. It is the business of the South, he maintained, to eliminate discrimination against the southern Negro, and until that table is overturned it remains their primary problem.

Again, we are responsible for demonstrating democracy at home, thereby most effectively commending it abroad. It seems doubtful that we can force it upon anybody, but we can recommend it mightily by showing its glory and its greatness. Dr. Ralph Bunche has been quoted in the newspaper as saying: "It is part of our strength that in the democratic framework of our society we are entitled to point to our shortcomings. Yet it is unfortunate that they are there. Our enemies, of course, exaggerate; we couldn't expect them to do otherwise. But to our friends, these imperfections are puzzling. It seems to me that our answer must be— and it is the only answer worthy of a democratic society —to exert every possible effort to eliminate undemocratic practices and undemocratic attitudes; to do all we can to close the gap between our professions of democracy and our practice of it."

Furthermore, it is our responsibility to wear our own armor in the battle of life, and not to try to wear that which belongs to somebody else. Edgar DeWitt Jones has written a sermon entitled "On Being Ourselves." In it he calls attention to that story in the Old Testament where Saul puts his armor on David, and David girds on the sword and clanks around in Saul's unwieldy armor. When he tries to take a step, he can hardly do it. Then he has the wisdom to lay it off and take up his own proper weapon—a slingshot (with which he was as expert, Dr. Jones remarks, as a cowboy is with a lasso). Thus he goes forth in his own way to the crucial battle. People sometimes try to put upon us armor which does not fit us. It is our responsibility to wear our own. Here is a mother, of whom one counselor tells, who wanted to be a singer, but was frustrated in that career. She transferred her ambition to her daughter, and poured into her susceptible imagination all of her own disappointed hopes and longings. The girl's imagination is captured and her conscience compelled with a sense that this is what she should do. Yet for her there is a complete chasm between her real abilities and that goal. Thus her life is disrupted, and there is no way out until she resolves to be herself and accept herself. We must go to the battle of life to do that for which we are responsible, not that for which somebody else is responsible.

Benefits

If along some such lines as these, we find what is a right Christian responsibility for ourselves, it will do us much good. It will take the strain off our hearts. Norman Vincent Peale described a man he knew as thinking that the world rested on his shoulders, and that his business and everything with which he was connected would fall apart if he did not personally take charge of every single detail. It was not the business, it was the man himself, who went to pieces under that pressure. But that sort of a load is taken off our hearts when we realize that while we have responsibility, other people have too. We extend a compliment and a challenge to others when we leave to them that which is properly theirs. In addition to that, we are actually enabled to accomplish more ourselves, precisely because we are concentrating upon that which is our own proper task. And this attitude represents faith in God himself. Who do we think we are anyway? Do we have to carry the whole universe by ourselves? Isn't God anywhere any more? Of course he is! He gives us a task fitted to our strength; it is our part to do it as well as we can and to trust him for the rest.

16. The Nonchalance
of Faith

The "nonchalance of faith" is a phrase once used by Reinhold Niebuhr, and the word of Paul which appropriately accompanies it, "Whether we live or whether we die, we are the Lord's,"[1] was also cited by him. The following story, however, is one which I am sure Dr. Niebuhr never told. It comes from the roundup in Wyoming and concerns a character who earned the title of "Nonchalant Pete."

On the roundup this morning he roped out a horse which was supposed to be an outlaw; therefore he saddled the horse very carefully, climbed on very cautiously, and rode most of the morning very alertly, expecting that there would be a tornado let loose underneath him at any moment. When that did not happen he began to think that the horse was overrated, and consequently he relaxed. As a matter of fact he had just struck a match, and this was the point for which the horse was waiting. Being in fact an outlaw, the bronco put his head between his legs and began to pitch and buck madly and blindly. He pitched so blindly that he went ahead in the direction of a deep arroyo and disappeared over the edge of this canyon. When the others came up to the edge, expecting to see catastrophe, they were amazed. Not far below the edge, a tree was growing out from the side of the canyon, and the horse was caught inextricably in its branches. Pete was still sitting in the saddle, and looking up he said, "Will someone give me a match? Mine blew out as we went over."

The English word *nonchalance* is derived from two French words, *non chaloir*, meaning "not to be concerned." It signifies an attitude of unconcern, of indifference to consequence, of imperturbability in peril.

Nonchalance in the Christian Faith

Although not often emphasized, the attitude of nonchalance belongs properly to the Christian faith. When Jesus was told that Herod Antipas was seeking to kill him, he sent back the answer, "Tell that fox, . . . I must go on my way."[2] When they led Jesus forth to Calvary to die, the women of Jerusalem, lining the street as he went, lamented and wept. He turned to them and said, "Do not weep for me, but weep for yourselves."[3] Ralph W. Sockman has commented that Jesus walked toward his death with such superb unconcern that his closest friends could not believe he was about to die.

Paul exhibited the nonchalance of the Christian faith when he wrote to the Romans, "Whether we live or whether we die, we are the Lord's."[4] He also wrote

to the Philippians and said, "I have suffered the loss
of all things, and count them as refuse, in order that I
may gain Christ."[5] The position he had once occupied,
the prestige he had enjoyed, the power he had had—
all of that he gave up to become an apostle of Christ.
If we had given up all of those things, many of us
would probably have gone on all the rest of our lives
feeling sorry for ourselves. But not Paul. He made
the sacrifice with the nonchalance which belongs to the
Christian faith. He said, in effect, "I have suffered
the loss of all things, but they were not anything anyway." The word used when he says they were refuse
is such a strong word in Greek that it is seldom translated literally, but Goodspeed preserves much of the
feeling of Paul's words when he renders: "I have lost
everything, and think it rubbish."[6] In the 1623 print-
ing of a folio of Shakespeare's works, there is a notation in the margin about the craftsman who did the
work. His name was Jaggard, and this remarkable
statement is made about him: "Nothing in his life
became him like leaving it. He died as one that had
been studied in his death. To throw away the dearest
things he own'd, as 'twere a careless trifle." That was
what Paul did. He threw away the dearest things he
owned for Christ, and said, "It was nothing anyway,
just a trifle."

Emil Brunner, one of the most eminent theologians
of our time, exhibits the nonchalance of the Christian
faith. When asked by *The Christian Century* for an
article on the subject, "What Can I Preach in Such a

Time as This?" it evidently seemed to him that the question implied a belief that this is a very bad time in which to preach the Christian gospel. Indeed, in many ways it does not appear to be a good time. There are large perils upon the horizon. One might be afraid. But see how Brunner waves this aside with a nonchalant spirit:

> If I understand it correctly, the question carries the implication that preaching is particularly difficult "in such a time as this." I am decidedly not of that opinion. Some years ago I proposed that an honorary D.D. degree be posthumously conferred on Adolf Hitler because no one had done so much for Christianity as he. . . . After Hitler came to power, it suddenly dawned on a great many people who theretofore had not bothered at all about Christianity that the stake in the fight against Hitler was nothing less than the foundations of our life, of our whole civilization.
>
> The same is true, and in even higher degree, with regard to communism today. The threat to the world represented by the politics of radical atheism has awakened us to the fact that atheism itself is a threat to all meaningful human life.
>
> In such a time as this we are conscious of the insecurity of our existence; and only when we feel insecure do we have room for the thought of God. Therefore this is a good time for finding God.[7]

Sources of Nonchalance

Now look at some of the things which Christianity gives men which enable them to have something of this nonchalance of faith. For one thing, Christianity helps us to have our main treasure in a safe place. Imagine a person who is away on his vacation. He receives word by telegram that thieves have broken into his house and ransacked it. He reads the telegram, and smiles and throws it in the wastebasket. That is possible because before his departure he took his chief treasures away and put them in the bank vault. He smiles to think that the burglar went to all that trouble to get in and then found only insignificant trinkets of relatively little worth. Christianity helps us put the emphasis upon the truly important things. Jesus says, "Do not lay up for yourselves treasures on earth, where moth and rust consume and where thieves break in and steal, but lay up for yourselves treasures in heaven, where neither moth nor rust consumes and where thieves do not break in and steal."[8]

Christianity helps us to make the inner citadel of life secure. Picture a military commander. Word comes to him that on the periphery, a minor fortification has fallen, an outer bastion has been taken. He is unperturbed as he receives this word, because he knows the immense strength in the inner fortifications. Christianity helps us to secure the inner citadel of life. Jesus says that we should not fear him who is able to kill the body and is not able to kill the soul, but fear only him who is able to destroy both body and soul in hell. If the center of life is secure, there can be a relative unconcern about the less important things. If things are all right at home, we can go out into the world and take the blows that come and stand up against them. If things are all right in the home of the mind, we can take outward blows with equanimity, or at any rate with the ability to recover balance after a blow. If things are all right where the soul is at home with God, then the things out on the edges can be taken with greater poise.

Christianity helps us to be prepared for life's emergencies by pre-prayer. No prayer is ever to be despised. If a man comes to a great emergency in his life, and has not prayed for many years, but then realizes his insecurity and his need of God and cries to God, God will surely hear him. But it is a good thing when people are prepared by prayer ahead of time for the emergencies which come. It is said that Dwight L. Moody was crossing the Atlantic ocean on one of his missions, when in midocean a terrific storm was encountered. The ship appeared to be in great danger. Most of the passengers became very anxious, and organized private or group prayer meetings. When Mr. Moody was asked why he was not praying like all the rest, he replied, "I'm all prayed up."

Handling Life's Difficult Assignments

Note, then, how men do in actual fact handle some of the difficult things in life this way, and how in this nonchalance there is something of very real faith although not always called by that name. People handle worry and overcome its insidious grip in this manner.

Do you remember the French soldier's litany of the first World War, with its philosophy on the futility of worry?

> You have two alternatives: Either you are mobilized or you are not. If not, you have nothing to worry about.
>
> If you are, you have two alternatives: Either you are in camp or at the front. If you are in camp, you have nothing to worry about.
>
> If you are at the front, you have two alternatives: Either you are in reserve or you are on the fighting line. If you are in reserve, you have nothing to worry about.
>
> If you are on the fighting line, you have two alternatives: Either you fight or you do not. If you do not, you have nothing to worry about.
>
> If you do, you have two alternatives: Either you get hurt or you do not. If you do not, you have nothing to worry about.
>
> If you do, you have two alternatives: Either you get slightly hurt or you get badly hurt. If slightly hurt, you have nothing to worry about.
>
> If badly, you have two alternatives: Either you recover or you do not. If you recover, you have nothing to worry about. If you do not and have followed my advice clear through, you have done with worry forever.

Men handle handicaps best with nonchalance. Harry Emerson Fosdick once told about a young man in his twenties who lost an arm. He decided to become an expert typist, and worked up to forty, fifty, and sixty words a minute. Then he attained seventy words a minute, and finally eighty. Someone asked him what he thought he could do if he had two hands, and he answered, "Not as much as eighty. The other hand would undoubtedly be in the way."[9]

Men go down with the flag flying, with something of that same nonchalance, and when they do they exhibit a real faith. Some years ago, the luxury liner "President Coolidge" docked in San Francisco, and Captain Dale E. Collins reported that a radio message had reached him from his friend Jack Welch, who was serving as skipper on the Chinese junk in which Richard Halliburton sought unsuccessfully to cross the Pacific. A typhoon had come, in which the "Coolidge" itself encountered waves fifty feet high and was slowed to six knots. Through the storm, across the miles, came Welch's message, the last that was ever received from Halliburton's junk: "Southerly gales. Rain squalls. Lee rail under water. Wet bunks, hardtack, bully beef. Having wonderful time. Wish you were here instead of me."

And that is how Christian faith handles death itself. There is something of the spirit of which we have spoken in the words of William E. Brooks:

> After the day they bury me
> I will nourish the roots of a cedar tree,
>
> And this that was I once more will pass
> Into meadow flowers and meadow grass;
>
> This that hungered, this that sang,
> Whose tears once fell, and whose laughter rang;
>
> This that thrilled to its hour of bliss,
> Leaning anew to a lover's kiss;

That warred in a war that men forget,
And strove for a peace that comes not yet;

Back again to the earth that gave,
Held, through the night, by a lonely grave;

Only to nourish grass and tree—
This is the cycle blind men see.

But I, whom they thought a buried clod,
Will have climbed the stars to talk with God![10]

17. How to Distinguish Right From Wrong

By what concrete methods can one tell the difference between right and wrong? Long ago the author of Proverbs declared: "There is a way which seems right to a man, but its end is the way to death."[1] That is the problem: How to tell, when you look at a way, whether it leads to life or to death, whether it is right or wrong.

Learning Too Late

There is, of course, one way of telling the difference between right and wrong: Go ahead and do the thing, and then see what results. Perhaps it is the experience of someone who has followed this method which is reflected in the proverb. Upon a superficial glance a way appears to be all right, but when you actually walk down it, you find that the end is death. If we wonder whether something is right or wrong, and have an uneasy feeling that it may be wrong, but want to see, we can go ahead and do it. Then if, after we have done it, we hate ourselves; if we reproach ourselves for our utter stupidity; if we loathe ourselves for our uncleanness and vileness; if we feel that there is a weight bearing down upon us, and a mark ineradicably impressed upon us; if we wake up in the night, shuddering to remember what we have done; if we cannot bear to think about it and yet cannot stop thinking about it— then we can be reasonably sure that what we have done was wrong instead of right.

This is one way to find the answer: Go ahead and do the thing.   Then, afterward, if you realize that you have done irreparable harm to somebody else, that you have betrayed a trust, have blighted an aspiration, have ruined a relationship—then you can be quite sure that it was the wrong thing instead of the right thing to do. Go ahead and do it, and if afterward you find that God is a stranger instead of a friend, and prayer is a cry of desperation instead of a conversation in quiet, then you can be sure that it was wrong.

Now it is obvious that this is not a very desirable way of finding out the difference between right and wrong. In one of his books, Leslie Weatherhead asks, "What is hell?" and answers with five points including a sense of deprivation from spiritual joy, a feeling of remorse, an experience of sorrow, a realization of the harm we have done others, and a progressive deterioration of character.   Much of this comes to pass even here and now if we mistake wrong for right and do it.   Are there not, therefore, tests by which we can tell ahead of time, and before it is too late, the difference between right and wrong?   Here are six.   To any single one there may perhaps be occasional exceptions, but taken all together and wisely applied, they will give us dependable guidance.

Six Tests

The first test is that of publicity. Would you like people generally to know about what you propose to do? If so, it is probably right. If you would prefer that people generally did not know about it, very possibly it is wrong. "Every one who does evil hates the light, and does not come to the light, lest his deeds should be exposed. But he who does what is true comes to the light, that it may be clearly seen that his deeds have been wrought in God."[2] If what you do, or think of doing, tends to make you skulk in the darkness, deceive those who are dearest to you, and avoid the light of day, then it is probably wrong. If it is something that belongs naturally in the light, it is probably right. Phillips Brooks wrote: "To keep clear of concealment, to keep clear of the need of concealment. . . . I cannot say how more and more that seems to me to be the glory of a young man's life. It is an awful hour when the first necessity of hiding anything comes. . . . Put off that day as long as possible. Put it off forever if you can."[3]

The second test is the test of universalization. This is to ask whether you would like to have people everywhere do what you are doing or thinking about doing. If you would, it is probably right. But if you would not like to have other people do what you are doing or thinking about doing, then it is probably wrong.

The philosopher Immanuel Kant stated this as the "categorical imperative," which is to "act as if the maxim of our action were to become by our will a universal law of nature." What is the principle involved in what I am going to do? If I could will to have that principle prevail everywhere, would I like it? If so, it is right. If the answer is no, the chances are it is wrong.

The third test is that of reciprocity. Would I like to have happen to me what I am going to cause to happen to somebody else? If I would, it is probably right, but if I would not want to have happen to me what I am going to cause to happen to somebody else, it is probably wrong. This principle was stated by Confucius of China around 500 B.C. in his well-known formulation: "Do not unto others what you would not they should do unto you."

The fourth test is the test of semantics. *Semantikos* is a Greek word denoting "significant meaning." Semantics is the modern science of the meaning of words. The semanticists claim that we cannot think clearly, logically, and well until we know what the words mean with which we think and with which we express our thoughts. That is surely true. Let us see if we can apply this test to the matter of determining the difference between right and wrong. If the real word for what we are proposing to do is an ugly word, the thing is probably wrong; if it is a beautiful word, the thing is probably right. We often dodge, in this matter, by rationalization. To rationalize is to think up an excuse afterward for what you have done already. That also includes employing a good word to gloss over a bad thing. This we very readily do. Emerson once said: "That which we call sin in others is experiment for us." Harry Emerson Fosdick picked that up and went on with it like this: "Where others lie, we are clever; where others cheat, we are shrewd and canny; where others are bad-tempered, we are righteously indignant; judging others, we would call their conduct selfish; judging ourselves, we call it practical."[4] The test of semantics is to get the word which really describes what we are, or do, or think to do. In writing to the Galatians, Paul says that the works of the flesh are plain, and then names some of them. As he uses the accurate word for each thing it is indeed plain that these things are wrong things: "immorality, impurity, licentiousness, idolatry, sorcery, enmity, strife, jealousy, anger, selfishness, dissension, party spirit, envy, drunkenness, carousing, and the like."[5]

The fifth test is that of relative difficulty. As a general principle it may be stated that the harder thing is more likely to be the right thing; and the easier, the wrong. In the realm of precious stones, we value most highly those that are hardest. In the realm of character, the matter is comparable. It seems to take difficult obstacles to bring out great character, and often we can tell the difference between alternatives, when puzzled, by asking: "Is this the path of least resistance?" If so, there is a good chance that it is the wrong path. "Is this the path that is harder to take?" If so, there is a good chance that it is the right one.

The sixth test is the test of the face of a friend. How does the matter seem when you look into the face of a friend? If it is something which makes you look into the face of your best friend with your eyes open, and a happy feeling in your heart, it is probably right. If it is something that makes you avoid the gaze of your best friend, and feel a little uncomfortable when you look at that person, then it is probably wrong. Thomas Mann, in his extended story of Joseph in Egypt, says that when Joseph faced his greatest temptation, the thing that saved him was the fact that the face of his father rose up before him. The New Testament tells of Peter and his lamentable denial of Christ with an oath, at the taunt of a slave girl. Afterward Jesus may have been led across the courtyard, and Luke states that he "turned and looked at Peter."[6] That was when, at the sight of the face of his Master, Peter realized what he had done, and rushing out wept bitterly. That was also the beginning of the way back for Peter.

In London, England, Quinton Hogg was a great benefactor of outcast boys. He was known familiarly and affectionately by his initials, Q. H. One of the wildest characters he ever tried to deal with was a certain Jem Nicholls. This man was later asked how he was getting along, and here is his answer: "I have a bit of trouble in keeping straight, but I thank God all is well. You see, I carry a photo of Q. H. with me always, and whenever I am tempted, I just take it out, and his look is a wonderful help, and by the grace of God I am able to overcome all."[7]

Results

What happens if we find the right, and do it? We saw at the outset that if we become confused on this matter, then confusion follows everywhere. If we call the right wrong, and call the wrong right, then everything in turn gets tangled up. We do the wrong, and everything goes wrong. Conversely, when we do the right, everything comes right. On the occasion of a recent visit to America, the philosophy of Albert Schweitzer, perhaps the greatest Christian thinker of our time, was presented in these words: "The fundamental question facing every human endeavor is not, 'Is it socially or economically promising, or comfortable, or beautiful?' but 'Is it right or wrong?' If it is right it will automatically lead to progress. It is precisely the loss of this ethical foundation—the growing lack of capacity for thinking about good and evil—which deprives contemporary culture of all sense of direction."[8]

The first and fundamental question in life, whether for a nation or for a man, is to ask, "Is it right or wrong?" If it is right, and we do it, then all things will be right.

18. Like the Feet of the Deer

Those who love animals, find themselves at home in the Bible. A veritable cavalcade of animals marches through its pages. Some of them are domestic animals: the ass, the donkey, the camel, the ox, the goat, the sheep, the dog, the horse. Some of them are the untamed creatures of wilderness and mountain: the crafty fox, the skulking jackal, the fleet gazelle, the wild goat, the roaring lion, the marauding wolf, the powerful hippopotamus, the lurking crocodile. Among them, too, is the animal mentioned in a passage found in almost identical wording in Psalm 18:33, 2 Samuel 22:34, and Habakkuk 3:19: "He made my feet like hinds' feet, and set me secure on the heights." The Hebrew word here is 'ayyalah, which is correctly translated in the Revised Standard Version as "hind." The hind is the female of the red deer, the male being the stag. In the case of the fallow deer, the female is called the doe. Doubtless because the latter word is more familiar, it is used in the American Translation. Since at all events it is a member of the deer family which is referred to, it is quite permissible simply to use the word "deer," and this is what is done in the Moffatt Translation.

What do the Biblical writers have in mind when they speak of having feet which are like the feet of the deer? They allude, evidently, to the sure-footedness of the deer, the ability of this animal to make its way with gentle, silent, precise steps through the forested glen, and more than that to go upon the high places and to pick its way over the uncertain rocks with certain steps. Have we not seen in the high mountains, a deer, going upon precarious places with sure steps, or bounding up and down the great slopes with illimitable energy? To the envy of us poor puffing, panting human beings, who go up and down those same rocky slopes with slow steps, the deer leaps up or down the mountainside as if its legs were made of springs of steel!

A mountain guide must also be sure-footed. Recall the ascent of the Weisshorn. This great white peak looms up above the village of Zermatt, a symmetrical pyramid of rock, covered with snow and ice. The party of climbers ascended far up the peak, and then came to the point where the only possible way ahead and above lay along a knife-edge of ice. The ice slopes fell off on either side at such an angle as to be utterly impossible to negotiate. They stood there and looked at it for a long time, then the leader turned his feet so that his toes pointed out, and set his first foot down with the middle of the foot right on the knife-edge of ice. He swung the other foot around with the toes pointed out, on the other side, and set it down on the knife-edge. Looking straight ahead and balancing himself with his ice ax, he walked across. The others followed.

Oh, for the feet of a great mountain guide, or the feet of a deer, that one might go with security upon the perilous, narrow places of life! That is what the Biblical writers are talking about.

Perilous Places

There are many places in life where we need to be able to walk in that way. The pathway of education is like that, because there is a slippery slope of neglect on one side and some youth never quite get up onto the trail. Other people slip off on the other side and become what the world calls "highbrow." They are of little value any more in common ordinary life, because somehow education has gone to their heads!

There is the matter of a balanced personality. That, too, is something like a narrow path, with a slippery slope on either side. On the one side there is the descent which leads to introversion, where you are all wrapped up in yourself. On the other side there is the corresponding peril of extreme extroversion, where you cannot endure it unless you are surrounded by other people all the time, and where you have no deep inner resources of your own. Balanced personality is found along the pathway between, and it is narrow.

True friendship is a narrow pathway. On the one hand you may become a hermit, and on the other you may be a "hail fellow, well met," who goes with the crowd on every occasion. A true friend stands sympathetically with another, yet maintains his own integrity.

Moral character is like this, too. On the one hand there is the abyss of asceticism, in which men punish and torture themselves needlessly and foolishly. On the other hand there is the abyss of libertinism, where men do anything they want, and soon do not want anything, because nothing seems worth while any longer.

Above all, Christian life is like this, according to the teaching of Jesus. He spoke about a strait gate and a narrow way which lead to life. How shall we think of the strait gate and the narrow way? One might be inclined to think about it as a narrow, cramped little gate which you have to squeeze in through; then, once you have entered, you find a high wall pressing in on you on either side. You are cramped and repressed, and life is fundamentally determined by negations and restrictions. But what if the narrow way of Christianity is more like a trail going up a mountainside? There is a point where you can no longer wander in the pleasant valley. If you are going to attain the summit you must proceed along a narrow ridge; that is the only way upward.

John Bunyan put it somewhat like that in his *Pilgrim's Progress*. In the description of Pilgrim's journey from the City of Destruction to the City of God, you will remember that the travelers came at last to the foot of the hill Difficulty. "I beheld then," wrote Bunyan, "that they all went on till they came to the foot of the hill Difficulty, at the bottom of which was a spring. There were also in the same place two other ways besides that which came straight from the gate, one turned to the left hand and the other to the right, at the bottom of the hill; but the narrow way lay right up the hill, and the name of the way is called Difficulty." Mr. Formalist and Mr. Hypocrisy were in the party at the time, and at that point Mr. Formalist went off on a pleasant side path which beckoned on one hand, and Mr. Hypocrisy went off on an attractive way which led off at the other side. They were never heard of again, for the alluring byways did not go to the City of God. The only way that led thither went at this point straight up a hill called Difficulty. The Christian life has its places which are like that, where it narrows in to a step ascent.

Promises

But the Biblical writers bring us not only a reminder of steep ascents but also a word of great assurance about them, when they declare that God will make our feet like deer feet, and set us on these high places. This must mean that God will give us an enthusiasm for the high places of life. When you see a wild animal in a cage, you cannot help feeling sadness that that animal, whose native place is the wooded glen of the great forest, or the crags of the high mountains, has to be behind bars. Yet some of us cage ourselves in with idleness and with evil, when we ought to be walking on higher places. The American Standard Version reads, "He setteth me upon *my* high places." By his native relationships, man belongs to the high places of God. God will give us an enthusiasm for the heights.

Again, the statement we are studying contains a promise that God will give us equilibrium. *That*, if you go upon the high places, is one of the most needed things, as it was needed by that mountain guide who crossed the narrow ridge of the Weisshorn with a sense of balance that was perfect. One needs that there, and one needs it anywhere. In the precarious places of life, who will give us equilibrium? By the promise of the Bible, God himself will give us the balance that we may walk safely on the perilous places.

Here, too, is God's promise that he will give us endurance. How that is needed, when the trail grows narrow and climbs steeply! God promises that we shall be able to run in the morning and continue to walk without fainting through the long afternoon.

If We Fall

Finally, it is necessary to remember that some of us stumble and slip and fall upon the perilous trails of life. It may be that the Psalm in which the statement about the feet of the deer is found, was written by David. He went upon some high places for his country and for his God, and he also slipped and fell terribly. When he did, however, he humbled himself before God. He repented and asked for forgiveness. Then

he was helped up and started along the way again.
Perhaps it was he who also sang of the divine guidance
he received throughout his life, in the Twenty-third
Psalm:

> The Lord is my shepherd; I shall not want.
> He maketh me to lie down in green pastures:
> He leadeth me beside the still waters.
> He restoreth my soul:
> He leadeth me in the paths of righteousness for his
>   name's sake.
> Yea, though I walk through the valley of the shadow
>   of death,
> I will fear no evil: for thou art with me;
> Thy rod and thy staff they comfort me.
> Thou preparest a table before me in the presence of
>   mine enemies:
> Thou anointest my head with oil;
> My cup runneth over.
> Surely goodness and mercy shall follow me all the
>   days of my life:
> And I will dwell in the house of the Lord for ever.[1]

Notes

Except as otherwise noted, Bible quotations are from the Revised Standard Version. Quotations from the Revised Standard Version and the American Standard Version are by permission of the Division of Christian Education of the National Council of the Churches of Christ in the United States of America.

Chapter 1. The Orbits of Life

[1] Jude 13, King James Version.
[2] Jude 12, King James Version.
[3] Psalm 84:11.

Chapter 3. The Realism of the Bible

[1] William F. Albright, *From the Stone Age to Christianity* (2d ed. 1946), p. 183. Quoted by permission of the publishers, The Johns Hopkins Press, Baltimore.
[2] American Standard Version.
[3] *The Man from Nazareth* (1949), p. 18. By permission of Harper & Brothers, New York.
[4] Quoted by permission of Professor Harris Franklin Rall.

Chapter 4. The Second Half of the Century

[1] Deuteronomy 30:19.
[2] In "This World," *San Francisco Chronicle,* December 4, 1949. By permission of Dr. Van Dusen.

Chapter 5. Religion: Confusionism

[1] John 9:25.
[2] Radio sermon, December 24, 1944. By permission of Dr. Fosdick.

Chapter 6.   *At Ease in Zion*

[1]Matthew 11:28.
[2]Amos 6:1.
[3]Amos 6:4-6.
[4]Exodus 19:15; 32:6.
[5]Matthew 25:26.
[6]Mark 14:41.
[7]Amos 6:6.
[8]Amos 6:1, *The Bible: An American Translation,* by J. M. Powis Smith and Edgar J. Goodspeed. Quotations from this translation are by permission of The University of Chicago Press.
[9]Amos 5:21.
[10]Wisdom of Sirach 38:31-34, *The Bible: An American Translation.*
[11]John 5:17.
[12]Philippians 4:10.
[13]Luke 18:13.

Chapter 7.   *They Had a Mind to Work*

[1]Nehemiah 3:5.
[2]2 Corinthians 8:3-5.

Chapter 8.   *Greater Things Than These*

[1]Matthew 11:4f.
[2]John 14:11.

Chapter 9.   *The Cost of Things*

[1]Luke 14:28.
[2]Numbers 32:23.

Chapter 10.   *The Price of Spiritual Power*

[1]Mark 9:29, King James Version.

Chapter *11*. *It Is Difficult to Be Different*

[1]Romans 12:2.

Chapter *12*. *Conscious and Unconscious Religion*

[1]Exodus 20:15, King James Version.
[2]Matthew 25:35f.
[3]Matthew 10:19.
[4]*When the Lamp Flickers* (1948), pp. 22f. Quoted by permission of Abingdon Press, New York and Nashville.

Chapter *13*. *The Inner Sources of Strength*

[1]John 4:32.
[2]John 4:34.

Chapter *14*. *Wait on the Lord*

[1]Psalm 27:14, King James Version.
[2]1 Samuel 13:5.
[3]1 Samuel 13:7.
[4]1 Samuel 13:12.
[5]Psalm 37:23, King James Version.
[6]James 1:4, King James Version.

Chapter *15*. *Responsibility, Ltd.*

[1]Genesis 4:9.
[2]John 21:20-22, King James Version.
[3]1 Timothy 5:13.

Chapter *16*. *The Nonchalance of Faith*

[1]Romans 14:8.
[2]Luke 13:32f.
[3]Luke 23:28.
[4]Romans 14:8.

[5]Philippians 3:8.

[6]Philippians 3:8, *The Bible: An American Translation.*

[7]In *The Christian Century,* July 11, 1951. By permission of the editor.

[8]Matthew 6:19f.

[9]Radio sermon, December 3, 1944. By permission of Dr. Fosdick.

[10]In *The Christian Century,* June 8, 1938. By permission of the editor.

Chapter 17. How to Distinguish Right From Wrong

[1]Proverbs 14:12; 16:25.

[2]John 3:20f.

[3]Quoted by Harry Emerson Fosdick, *Twelve Tests of Character* (1923), p. 46. By permission of Association Press, New York.

[4]*On Being a Real Person* (1943), p. 138. By permission of Harper & Brothers, New York.

[5]Galatians 5:19-21.

[6]Luke 22:61.

[7]Harry Emerson Fosdick in Stanley I. Stuber and Thomas C. Clark, eds., *Treasury of the Christian Faith* (1949), p. 393. By permission of Association Press, New York.

[8]Winthrop Sargeant in *Life,* July 25, 1949, p. 80. By permission of the editors.

Chapter 18. Like the Feet of the Deer

[1]King James Version.

248.4
F49

Lincoln Christian College

74729